The World of BIG BANDS

The Sweet and Swinging Years

ARTHUR JACKSON

Foreword by Edmund Anderson

DAVID & CHARLES

NEWTON ABBOT . LONDON . VANCOUVER

ISBN 0 7153 7359 5

Set in 10 on 12 Goudy Old Style
and printed in Great Britain
by The Alden Press, Oxford
for David & Charles (Publishers) Limited
Brunel House   Newton Abbot   Devon

Published in Canada
by Douglas David & Charles Limited
1875 Welch Street   North Vancouver   BC

CONTENTS

FOREWORD

by EDMUND ANDERSON

If you are young enough to be of the generation that tingled to the beat of the Big Bands, their vocalists and the music they played, Arthur Jackson's *The World of Big Bands* is for you. If you are old enough to wonder about the popular music that preceded the current groups engendered by the likes of the Rolling Stones and the Beatles, etc, Mr Jackson's book is your singing, swinging cup of tea. If you are fascinated by the history of the Big Bands because of fact and statistics, it's all right here. If you're interested in the story of the Big Bands because of nostalgia, tender memories and sentiment, that's here too.

The volume of research and knowledge that Jackson brings to his subject is awesome. He has really done his homework. The book is filled with information of all sorts, some of it most unexpected and somewhat startling. For instance, were you aware that Will Osborne (an almost forgotten musical facsimile of leader-crooner Rudy Vallee) was the son and heir of a Scottish Baron? And did you know that comedian Art Carney was, in his youth, a member of a Horace Heidt vocal trio? Well, I didn't know those things and I thought I knew my way around the popular music world of the period. The book is peppered with these little nuggets of interest as well as the big important ones.

I was personally involved with some of the goings on during the hey-day of the bands and, therefore, I feel qualified to enjoy the author's chronicle. The largest of the soft drink companies in America for several years sponsored a radio programme five nights a week called 'The Spot Light Bands', featuring a different name band every night, thereby rotating the appearance of just about every important band in the country. I was a broadcast director-writer on that series and travelled all over the country to pick up the various groups on location. (Some of the music I loved, and some grated indeed.) I have also worked in various other capacities with many of the people Jackson talks about in the fields of broadcast, recording and theatre. My number one hero, Duke Ellington, recorded the very first song I ever helped to write and later stood at my side when I married. My children still call Ray Noble 'Uncle Ray'.

It's all here, the histories of Benny Goodman, the Dorsey brothers, Jack Hylton, Louis Armstrong, Ted Heath, Paul Whiteman, the Duke, the Count, Glenn Miller and Ambrose . . . from Harlem to Hammersmith. Included are the vocalists of the bands, Bing Crosby, Frank Sinatra, Rosemary Clooney, Perry Como, Al Bowlly and many of the others who started as band singers.

And the songs! The motion picture companies and their captively owned music publishers fed the bands much of the material. Writing for the stage and pictures in the twenties, thirties and forties were the Gershwins, Jerome Kern, Harry Warren, Harold Arlen, Johnny Mercer, Cole Porter, *et al*. Oh, the quality of the songs we were constantly exposed to! The boys had something to play and many of the arrangers for the big bands were brilliant. It was indeed the best time for popular music.

Mr Jackson covers not only the American scene extensively but goes into great detail with the British orchestras and, to some extent, the continental groups as well. If your interest lies only with the Americans you can skip the English and the Europeans and get your money's worth. If you're curious about the English and continentals and not the Americans, the same applies. As for me, I devoured it all.

Some years ago Ellington recorded an LP album titled 'Will the Big Bands Ever Come Back?', a group of musical reworkings of the music of some of the popular Big Bands. The record is now out of press but the question remains.

INTRODUCTION

Big bands are finished, they tell us. They won't come back. The ballrooms that once resounded to eight brass and five saxes now tremble under the kilowattage of pop groups or the soulless turntables of the discotheque which has, all too often, replaced live entertainment. So why bother to write a book about a dead art?

But there is another school of thought which maintains that big bands are coming back, pointing to the handful of dance and swing bands that still function on borrowed time, the last few hold-outs from a vanished era. This may be wishful thinking, but the truth is probably somewhere between the two opposing viewpoints. True, the big band scene is moribund insofar as modern entertainment is concerned, but the endless reissues of recordings of dance and swing music from the halcyon years of the 1930s and 1940s indicate that interest in the music itself is still very much alive, and that maybe only a matter of practical economics keeps the bands off the road.

It would be nice to think that one day it could happen again. It won't, of course, but there can be little harm in thinking nostalgically of happier days, in wanting them to return. And surely the key word is nostalgia? This is an element which exists in all of us as an integral part of our makeup, however much it may be denied by the more pragmatic. It could hardly be otherwise, since so much of our lives is bound up with music in one form or another (even today's thirty year olds look back nostalgically to the early rock and roll era of the mid-1950s, which to them is 'the good old days'). A favourite record that recalls events and places, a song that meant something very personal to two people, or may be a band that one danced to on a special occasion—all these associations of ideas culminating in a heart-warming sensation have little to do with practical considerations.

And for those of a certain generation, possibly a larger one than is generally realised, they add up to an appreciation, whether for reasons nostalgic or purely musical, of dance bands which, from the 1920s right through to the advent of the rock and pop era, were the principal interpreters of the popular music of the day. The top bands had their regular radio spots, either from the studios or on location from hotels and ballrooms, and the leaders were the prime target of the song-pluggers, who knew that one peak-hour broadcast on a new song by a leading band was a guarantee of nationwide success for the sheet music. Bandleaders themselves were the pop stars of their day with a tremendous personal following, while the band vocalists earned great reputations which were often the foundation of successful solo careers. Bands of all types—sweet, swinging, exotic, comic; those built upon a foundation of visual showmanship or those dedicated to pure jazz—were predominant in hotels, ballrooms, restaurants, night clubs, films, and on stage, radio and records.

Particularly on records! Incredible though it may seem in the present musical climate, there was a time when swing bands dominated 'the charts'. In July 1940, for example, the USA Top Ten consisted of three records by Glenn Miller, two by Tommy Dorsey, and one each from the bands of Jimmy Dorsey, Kay Kyser, Charlie Barnet and Mitchell Ayres (the odd one out was Bing Crosby, who at that time had his own permanent spot reserved in the Top Ten anyway). Is it any wonder, then, that so many of us who were constantly exposed to this music in our formative years should have retained a lifelong devotion to big bands that stays with us however widely our musical interests expand in other directions as we progress through maturity?

My own interest has always been complete and avid, though not quite life-long. There were a few wasted years at the outset and I must have been all of ten before I took any interest in dance music, at a time when the BBC treated me nightly to the sounds of Harry Roy at the Café Anglais, Ambrose at the Embassy Club, Jack Jackson at the Dorchester Hotel, and Jack Payne and the BBC Dance Orchestra in the studio. Seeing my first 'name' band in the flesh when Lew Stone and his band appeared in cine-variety at the Paramount Theatre in Newcastle when I was twelve gave me a dedication to the big band sound which endures to the present day.

Hence this book which will, I hope, be a means of sharing my memories and enthusiasms with others of similar persuasion. I can't guarantee a completely impartial report. 'The Golden Age of Dance Bands', 'The Swing Era', or whatever you choose to call your favourite period in big band music, produced a lot of excellent music, but there were, as in any period of time, mediocre bands and bad songs. But as is always the case in any form of entertainment (in fact, in any sort of human experience), the bad is forgotten and the good survives, but all of it must be documented to present a comprehensive picture of the scene. Objectivity should be the name of the game, but musical appreciation is a wholly subjective thing anyway, and the reader must allow the author to indulge his own enthusiasms and prejudices. Just a little, mind you—perhaps a slight over-emphasis on a particular favourite or a fractionally more cursory look at one less favoured.

Incidentally, this might be a good time to mention that in the context of this book the term 'big bands' is going to mean just what you want it to mean; anything and everything from the syrupy saxophones of Guy Lombardo to the screaming riffs of Lionel Hampton, from the dexterous chamber jazz of the Goodman Trio to the weighty ensemble of Paul Whiteman, from the luxuriant strains of the Hawaiian bands to the musical lunacy of Spike Jones. It is obviously impossible, nor is it desirable, to cover fully the activities of every band which formed a part of dance music history over the past sixty years, nor even to mention them all. My brief is to present a rounded picture of the world of big bands in all its various aspects, bringing out the highlights and musical milestones, the best-known and most influential names among the bandleaders, singers, musicians and arrangers as I remember them. As we all remember them, with respect, admiration and affection.

1 IN THE BEGINNING THE EARLY YEARS

Any attempt to trace the history of dance music right back to its roots would involve a journey of several thousand miles in distance and as many years in time, for as far as is known the earliest type was that which accompanied Chinese and Balinese tribal dancing. Dance music and dancing probably first moved into the ballroom around the sixteenth century to the rhythms of the pavane and gaillard, which were followed in succeeding centuries by the gavotte, minuet, courante, cotillon, allemande etc. Dancing of this type was the province of the upper classes, the orchestras often being hidden from sight in the minstrels' galleries still to be found in country houses of the stately homes variety. It was not until about 150 years ago that dancing became a public affair with the popularisation of the waltz, polka, mazurka and other dances, usually of continental origin. I suppose that if one cares to regard it in such a light, the first 'name' big band leader was Johann Strauss I who, like his even more famous son, was very much a working musician and conductor. Over a century later bandleader Wayne King of Chicago's Aragon Ballroom was known coast-to-coast as 'the Waltz King'; but Strauss has prior claim to the title.

Dance music as we know it today began in and around Chicago before World War I, and the Windy City was pulsating with musical activity around 1911–12. In view of the nature of dance bands at that time 'pulsating' may not be the *mot juste*, but certainly there was employment for musicians and bands: at the Fountain Inn for violinist Charlie Elgar, at the Pekin Theatre for clarinettist Wilbur C. Sweatman, at the Rainbow Gardens for pianist Charlie Straight. There were others like Earl Dabney at New York's Ziegfeld Roof, and Chicago leader Erskine Tate (later resident at the Vendome Theatre with Louis Armstrong in his trumpet section), but popular legend does generally credit Wilbur Sweatman with having the first organised dance band. His moment of glory was brief, and if he is remembered nowadays it is as the composer of 'Down Home Rag' and for the fact that he once had a twenty-one year old pianist named Duke Ellington.

One of the more reputable bands of the period was formed in San Francisco in 1913 by Art Hickman for a residency at the St Francis Hotel. Hickman, composer of 'Rose Room', was one of the first leaders to experiment with a larger instrumentation; and it is pertinent to recall that dance band arrangements were still some years in the future, along with developments like brass, saxophone and rhythm sections. Violin and cornet, and occasionally a trombone, formed the usual front line, with piano, banjo and drums bringing up the rear. It's difficult to define dance music of this period. Imagine a cross between ragtime and brass bands, with a flavouring of salon music, with routines worked out over a copy of sheet music. Hickman's band, which at various times included Roy Fox and Bert Ralton, made the St Francis Hotel their almost permanent home until 1919, when Florenz Ziegfeld booked them for the Biltmore Hotel and his own Ziegfeld Roof in New York. Hickman occupies a particular niche in history, his appearance in *The Ziegfeld Follies* being the first time a dance band had ever played on stage in a Broadway show. His New York success was such that he sent a second band to London in 1920 where, as Art Hickman's New York London Five, they played at the Roof Garden of the Criterion Restaurant. Meanwhile the main orchestra returned to the West Coast, but Hickman retired shortly afterwards and died in San Francisco in 1930 at the early age of forty-four.

These, then, were the pioneers in American dance music, which began several years ahead of the British variety. Even then, dance music in Britain was originated by American bands visiting London during World War I. One of the first among these was Murray

9

Pilcer's American Sherbo Sextette, which played at Maison Lyons in Oxford Street, the Oxford Theatre, Trocadero Restaurant and Savoy Hotel. The latter venue, later to assume an important role in British dance music, also featured Joe Wilbur's Savoy Quartet with pianist Dave Comer, best remembered for his composition 'Hors d'oeuvres', originally a piano solo but later a dance band standard in Sid Phillips's familiar orchestration. Without leader-singer-banjoist Wilbur, the group, which had been resident for some time at Murray's Club in London, also recorded as Murray's Ragtime Trio. Will Marion Cook's Southern Syncopated Orchestra (its personnel included Sidney Bechet) visited London during the war years and performed at Philharmonic Hall, and Cook returned after the war with his Rag-A-Jazz Band, but with less success, and when some of its members returned to America the band was reformed with British musicians. But of all the American visitors in those early years the most influential by far was the Original Dixieland Jazz Band. Formed in New Orleans in 1914, and known there and in Chicago two years later as Brown's Band, the ODJB gained its new name in 1917 while at Reisenweber's Restaurant in New York. The band came to England in 1919 to play the London Hippodrome, followed by club dates and an engagement for the opening of the Hammersmith Palais de Danse which has long since passed into the history books. More than fifty years after the event, purists still argue the ODJB's place in jazz and the claims of its volatile trumpeter Nick La Rocca to have invented jazz. However suspect the pretensions of a white band (although indigenous to New Orleans) to be authentic interpreters of what was then strictly black music, there can be no doubting the impact the ODJB made in a country whose first taste of jazz this was.

The band was as great an influence in its way and its time as was the invasion of American musicians in the Glenn Miller and Sam Donahue service bands in World War II. For dance music, or swing—call it what you will—has, as an offshoot of jazz, no matter how many times removed, always been an essentially American idiom which British and continental bands have necessarily followed. This does not imply that non-American music was always second-hand. As we shall see later, Britain, and to a lesser extent France and Germany, did produce worthwhile music devoid of outside influences. But it has been a general practice for American bands and musicians to set the styles. So it's hardly surprising that when a real, live American jazz band was heard in Britain for the very first time the imitators were out in force. But the ODJB presented Dixieland jazz for public consumption with a great deal of showmanship and extra-musical effects which, in most cases, were copied by British groups without too much regard for the basics of the jazz they embellished. Again, those musicians who were influenced for the better by the New Orleans jazz men had little opportunity to display their new-found interest in public. Jazz was still very suspect. 'Jungle music' was the term of denigration generally used, even up to the days of Duke Ellington's Cotton Club orchestra, and not even the critical praise and sponsorship of Sidney Bechet and the Southern Syncopated Orchestra by no less a personage than Ernest Ansermet, the conductor of L'Orchestre de la Suisse Romande, could make a dent in the typical British prejudice. Those musicians whose minds were full of new ideas had perforce to continue churning out the archetypal dance-cum-salon music which was the staple fare of the time.

In America the war and postwar years saw the emergence of not only the popular bands of the period—long forgotten names like Art Landry, Earl Fuller, Joseph C. Smith, Vincent Rose, Bert Lown, Herb Wiedoft et al—but also many men who were to become big time bandleaders of the twenties and thirties, from King Oliver's Olympia Band to more commercially minded men like Paul Specht, Emil Coleman, George Olsen, Vincent Lopez, Ted Lewis, Fred Waring, Meyer Davis, Ben Bernie, Jan Garber, Red Nichols, Sam

More vaudevillian than jazzman,
Ted Lewis overshadowed many
fine musicians in his band with his
corny clarinet and hammy singing,
but remained a favourite entertainer
until his death in 1971 in his
eightieth year.

Lanin, Johnny Hamp and Joe Kayser, all of them starting their careers in various parts of the United States. So, in 1918, did a twenty-eight year old viola player from the San Francisco Symphony Orchestra, named Paul Whiteman, who had been enraptured by the sounds of jazz and filled with an ambition to play it. During World War I Whiteman joined John Tait's band, but the engagement lasted exactly one day when Tait found that his new sideman's enthusiasm for jazz was not matched by any ability to play it. In 1917 Whiteman was turned down for the US army as overweight, but was later employed in the navy as a bandleader. Back in civilian life he formed a band for the Fairmont Hotel in San Francisco, and played dates in and around Los Angeles before settling in at the Hotel Alexandria in that city at the end of 1919. As pianist he had Ferde Grofe, a man his own age whom he had met during his fateful day with the John Tait band, and who had been experimenting with the idea of orchestrating dance music, a completely new departure for the busking bands which had been functioning so well for many years. Grofe had also been a viola player (with the Los Angeles Symphony) before concentrating on piano, and he joined Whiteman purely in this capacity; but after three years he handed the piano chair over to a succession of pianists including embryo conductors Roy Bargy, Lennie Hayton and Ray Turner, and devoted his time to composing and arranging for the orchestra. Apart from his own famous suites ('Grand Canyon', 'Mississippi', 'Hudson River' etc) and songs like 'Wonderful One' and 'Daybreak', Grofe was also responsible for the orchestration of George Gershwin's 'Rhapsody in Blue' which Paul Whiteman commissioned, and premiered at Aeolian Hall in 1924.

If I appear to be laying more emphasis on Whiteman and Grofe than on other contemporary leaders it is because their importance cannot be over-estimated. They took dance music out of the cornet-sax-fiddle-banjo-sousaphone stage and gave it full instrumental sections with an advanced form of orchestration that gave dance music an almost symphonic aspect. Let's admit at this point that Paul Whiteman had little to do with jazz *per se*, other than by his employment of such jazz musicians as Bix Beiderbecke, Jack Teagarden, Jimmy and Tommy Dorsey, Frankie Trumbauer, Joe Venuti, Red Norvo and Eddie Lang, even though these key men were all too often buried in the ensemble of the 'symphonic jazz' of this erroneously named 'King Of Jazz'. But we must remember that Whiteman was primarily a showman whose audience was the wider public rather than the jazz buffs. It is enormously to his credit that he did give steady work to such men even though some may have been a trial to him as an employer. He had great patience with the talented and tragic Bix, and it is perhaps poetic justice that any sale which Whiteman records may have nowadays is due almost entirely to Bix's presence. It was Paul Whiteman who did much to improve the standard of musicianship in dance bands, to encourage arrangers, star good

The 'King of Jazz' may have been
press agents' hyperbole, but **Paul
Whiteman's** (*centre below*) influence
on symphonic dance music was
undeniable, as was his sponsorship of
new talent. **Bing Crosby** (*top left*)
and **Mildred Bailey** sang their first
songs with 'Pops', and **Jack
Teagarden** (*bottom left*) and **Joe
Venuti** (*top right*) were among the
star jazzmen featured in the band.
(*RCA Records, New York; Capitol
Records; EMI Records*)

singers—Bing Crosby and the Rhythm Boys, Mildred Bailey, Johnny Mercer, Red McKenzie, Ken Darby, Morton Downey, the Modernaires etc—and in general herald the age, not only of big bands as such, but of such popular orchestras as those of André Kostelanetz, David Rose, Percy Faith, Robert Farnon, Paul Weston, Victor Young, Frank Chacksfield, Gordon Jenkins and the many others who combined legitimate orchestral techniques with dance band instrumentation in superior performances of popular music.

Whiteman's most direct influence at the time was on a man who was to become Britain's greatest musical showman. Jack Hylton began his career in 1909 at the age of seventeen when, after singing and playing piano in concert parties, he became conductor for a touring pantomime. Working his way from Bolton to London, young Hylton became a cinema

Jack Hylton, musical showman supreme. (*World Records*)

organist then, in 1914, relief pianist with Stroud Haxton's band at the 400 Club. After a return to concert party work during the war he was engaged as intermission pianist at the Queen's Hall Roof. Then the first Whiteman records arrived in London and came as a considerable surprise to London musicians, who were still 'playing it by ear'. As the only man at Queen's Hall who could read and write music and to have had conducting experience, Hylton was given the leadership of the Queen's Hall Orchestra with the specific assignment of creating musical sounds to match those of Paul Whiteman. His records in this vein were a huge success and Jack Hylton's Orchestra as it was by now known (he was allowed his name on the label in lieu of an extra fee for leading the band) progressed to increasingly important London venues. By 1929 he had achieved the sort of recording reputation that would make today's Gold Disc winners look ridiculous (it's said that in December 1929 alone he sold 6 million records). As the band grew larger Hylton decided to forego hotel work and turn it into a stage attraction, and he devoted the rest of his career to presenting big band music on stage with a flair for visual appeal that has seldom been equalled. But there was always a sound musical basis to all Jack Hylton's work thanks to the arrangements of multi-instrumentalist Billy Ternent, and on one notable occasion the Hylton band was augmented on tenor sax by Coleman Hawkins in a Fletcher Henderson arrangement of 'Darktown Strutters Ball', a performance indistinguishable from that of any top American swing band. When the call-up of musicians in World War II made it impossible for Jack Hylton to maintain his own high standards, he disbanded and went on to become Britain's leading theatrical impresario.

Meanwhile, back in Chicago two of the outstanding bands of the day were the Benson Orchestra at the Marigold Gardens and the Coon-Sanders Nighthawks at the Blackhawk Restaurant. The former was the brain child of Edgar A. Benson, a band agent whose own contribution to music may have been minuscule, but whose appointment of, initially, Roy Bargy and subsequently Don Bestor as musical director of 'his' band showed an acute combination of business sense and musical know-how. The Coon-Sanders band was formed by drummer Carlton A. Coon and pianist Joe L. Sanders who were also composers of some repute, and with four brass, three saxes and four rhythm the band purveyed an unpretentious but musicianly form of dance music for many years. An interesting sidelight is that Mel Tormé is said to have sung with this band at the age of four. Like Edgar Benson, some of the active bandleaders of the early twenties were actually music contractors who provided bands for society dances, one night stands, resident engagements and recording sessions under a variety of pseudonyms. Typical of this ilk were Ben Selvin, Meyer Davis, Sam Lanin (and in later years his brothers Lester and Howard), Ed T. Kirkeby and—probably the most outstanding in terms of musical excellence—Jean Goldkette. A Frenchman who came to America in 1910, Goldkette began as pianist at Lamb's Café in Chicago,

The original **Jean Goldkette band** (with Bix *et al*) had a short life in the twenties. This 1959 version with Goldkette fronting Swing Era veterans like Toots Mondello, Yank Lawson, Jimmy Maxwell, Will Bradley, Urbie Green, and Felix Orlewitz recreating Joe Venuti's violin solos, revived some of the old scores for an RCA Camden stereo album. (*RCA Records, New York*)

later moving to Detroit where he took over the Graystone Ballroom. He had a number of bands operating under his name, but as well as run-of-the-mill dance bands he organised one of the finest big bands of the decade, which included the Dorseys, Joe Venuti, Danny Polo, Frankie Trumbauer and Bix Beiderbecke (many of Bix's records under his own name were made with colleagues from the Goldkette band), with arrangements by Russ Morgan and Bill Challis. That the music was better than most of its period was proved in 1959 when the leader assembled an all-star band to recreate some of his old scores in stereo.

One thing we should remember is that most of these early bands depended for their reputations on personal appearances, hence such reputations were in some cases purely local. The record industry, for such of the bands as were lucky enough to be making records, was in its infancy without the worldwide, or even nationwide, distribution that pertains today. Again, acoustic recording in the pre-electric days was primitive to say the least. Comedian Jimmy Durante's New Orleans Jazz Band was one of the few early groups able to compete with the ODJB, and Durante himself was no mean ragtime pianist, leading his band at the Alamo Club in Harlem. He was later the guiding spirit behind the Memphis

Rudy Vallee, leader of the Connecticut Yankees, was the very first 'swoon crooner' back in the twenties. This is how film and TV fans see this distinguished light comedy actor nowadays. (*Warner Bros. Pictures*)

Five and Eddie and Sugar Lou's Orchestra. One of the true pioneers of jazz recording, Durante once told me: 'We couldn't use drums in those days. The recording machine couldn't take the vibrations—it would send the needle off the record. Imagine recording a Dixieland outfit without drums! Just trumpet, clarinet and trombone, with me supplying the whole rhythm section from piano!'

So the advent of radio became the greatest possible boon to the band business. There can be no sure way of knowing who were actually the first bands to broadcast, but it is generally accepted that Paul Specht and his orchestra gave dance music its first airing in Detroit in 1920, while in Britain the first dance music went out at 9pm on 23 December 1922, programmed merely as 'Orchestra—Dance Music' with songs by a bass singer, Harold Mann. The first named band to broadcast on the BBC was that of Marius B. Winter in February 1923, who paved the way for the regular broadcasts a few months later by the Savoy Hotel bands. (So important was the Savoy in dance music that it is dealt with in detail in the next chapter.) As radio spread across America, and especially with the establishment of the NBC coast-to-coast network in 1926, it offered tremendous exposure to dance bands. Two of those which gained early prominence were Lawrence Welk (Welk, as we will see later, was still going strong on TV over thirty years later, outliving most of the opposition) who had a small band with a regular spot on station WNAX in South Dakota, and the Coon-Sanders Nighthawks, featured regularly on remotes from the Blackhawk Restaurant in Chicago where they were succeeded by the bands of Hal Kemp and Kay Kyser. Guy Lombardo and his Royal Canadians were first heard on the air from Cleveland, Ohio, before moving to the Granada Cafe, Chicago, where their radio fame led to their permanent removal to the Roosevelt Hotel Grill in New York. By 1927 Duke Ellington was being heard direct from the Cotton Club, and Wayne King's smooth blend of saxophone and 3/4 tempi from the Aragon Ballroom in Chicago earned him the title of 'The Waltz King'.

The biggest show business name to be created in the early days of radio was Rudy Vallee. After playing saxophone with the Savoy Orpheans in London, Vallee returned to New York and formed his Connecticut Yankees to move into the Heigh-Ho Club, where his broadcasts over station WABC (heralded by his call of 'Heigh-ho everybody') soon made him one of America's greatest attractions, although less for the band's playing than for his own singing. Five years earlier than Bing Crosby, and a whole generation ahead of Frank Sinatra, Vallee was the first 'swoon crooner', though it's difficult at this date to see what the attraction was about his nasal, expressionless vocalising. To be quite fair about it, however, the standard of band vocalists in the twenties and early thirties was pretty dire, and in this context Vallee may well have been outstanding. A year later, in 1929, he commenced his famous *Fleischmann Hour* series which in turn led him to Broadway fame in George White's *Scandals* and Hollywood stardom. He was succeeded at the Heigh-Ho by Will Osborne, a Canadian, who, as the son of Lord Oliphant, was the heir to the Barony of Gask in Scotland. There was some controversy going at the time as to whether Osborne or Vallee was the first crooning bandleader, but while Vallee concentrated on his singing, Osborne's was probably the better band and he remained a consistent, if never spectacular, figure through to the mid-forties when he wound up in the studios as conductor on the Abbott and Costello radio show—but still playing sweet music for dances on the side. One of the most popular radio bands, although more in the mature years of the thirties than in those toddling days, was that of Ben Bernie, 'The Old Maestro', who after five years at the Hotel Roosevelt in New York, started his regular broadcasting schedule from Chicago's Sherman Hotel in 1929. Of all the names made by radio, Bernie's must be one of the most eminent. But not the earliest. So many dance bands were beginning to achieve nationwide fame on radio; but we must not overlook Vincent Lopez, whose broadcasts from his own Club Lopez, the Hotel Pennsylvania and the Taft Hotel, all in New York, gave a big boost to well-arranged and smoothly performed dance music.

Within the next few years, of course, radio would be a common place and dance music one of its main commodities, whether from the studios or direct from hotels and ballrooms. In America and Britain alike the sophisticated atmosphere of the top people's haunts was enjoyed vicariously in the humblest of homes via the magic of the cat's whisker and subsequent technological developments. And if, as in many cases, the sound of cutlery and plates or of the dancers' shuffling feet vied with the music, well, that was all part of the sense of occasion. With one or two exceptions the big bands had not yet completely arrived. But they were on their way. The pioneers of orchestration, the showmen who gave dance music its 'personalities', the alert minds that saw what big business dance music could become, the musicians who were improving their techniques, all were, whether they realised it or not at the time, leading the bands towards the Swing Era and the Golden Age of Dance Bands. Those are the times that people remember, the days when nostalgia begins. The halcyon years when, or so it seems in retrospect, it was always summertime and the living was easy and the music sweet and swinging. Perhaps it wasn't really like that at all, but we were young then.

It may be felt that my treatment of The Early Years has been somewhat perfunctory and less detailed than the chapters which follow. This may well be so, for a variety of reasons. Other books have dealt with those years in far greater detail, emphasising the general practitioners as well as the specialists I've introduced and, apart from the duplication of facts, I would never even try to compete with the scholarship of Messrs Rust and McCarthy, who have said it all. Again, for most of us, any study of the very early years is necessarily a purely academic exercise. Nevertheless this study, cursory though it may be, is essential to document the milestones in the history of our music, for only by a knowledge of what has gone before can we begin to appreciate subsequent developments.

The final, and perhaps most important point is that, with very few exceptions, the music of the pre-1930 years just hasn't endured. Occasional 'vintage' record reissues reveal, in the main, a corny, raw and generally uninteresting form of dance music that has little appeal. All music is dated, true, but the best of big band music from the succeeding decades, although dated, retains a musical validity in a way that this embryo music does not. This is a purely subjective point of view, of course, with which the reader is at liberty to disagree.

2 THE GOLDEN AGE THE THIRTIES

As the Roaring Twenties made way for the Tranquil Thirties the world of big bands began to take shape, although the mass of corny ragtimey bands of the twenties didn't change overnight into smooth, sophisticated and swinging orchestras. There was a transitional period with an increased emphasis on arrangements, an extra trumpet or sax added here and there. This mirrored the development of popular music itself, for although by the twenties Cole Porter had already brought sophistication into Broadway music with 'What Is This Thing Called Love?' and 'You Do Something To Me', although Gershwin's life

Isham Jones created some of the richest sweet music of the early thirties. His band was later taken over by Woody Herman. (*RCA Records, New York*)

and career were more than half over and Irving Berlin had written his greatest hits, it was in the area of the ordinary popular song that the greatest change came. Writers like Walter Donaldson and De Sylva, Brown and Henderson, who epitomised the twenties, gave way to the more polished and harmonically adventurous melodies of Harold Arlen, Harry Warren, Jimmy Van Heusen, Kurt Weill and Gordon Jenkins, and this was reflected in the playing of the bands which performed the songs as the hits of the day. True, 'Yes We Have No Bananas' was succeeded by 'Three Little Fishes', and nonsense and novelty songs were wished on bands and singers in ever-increasing numbers. But overall the thirties was a peak period for 'quality' songs—and quality bands.

Although I have separated the Swing Era and the Golden Age of Dance Bands there are no clearcut demarcation lines. The swing bands played for dancing, while most of the dance bands included a proportion of swing style instrumentals, some matching the accredited swing bands for musical excellence. Their main function, however, was to play commercial dance music for a living, which they did in varying degrees of style, flair and originality. Inspired by Fletcher Henderson, Duke Ellington and the Casa Loma Orchestra, more prominent American bands were going in for swing music, and among those remaining many were the society orchestras and 'mickey mouse' bands detailed in Chapter 6. Certainly the best British dance bands of the early thirties were superior to the average American group. But there were exceptions, and the leading American band was that of Isham Jones, one of the few leaders to have adopted a more progressive policy towards arrangements and the foundation of an identifiable style in the previous decade. It has been claimed that in 1931–5 Jones led one of the finest dance bands of all time, with a rich ensemble sound achieved through the arranging of Gordon Jenkins, Joe Bishop and Victor Young. But the catalyst blending musicians and arrangements in a completely

Al Bowlly. (*Music for Pleasure*)

satisfying musical entity was Isham Jones himself. Like Glenn Miller in later years Jones was a martinet disliked by his men, who nevertheless respected his ability as a musical director, as the focal point of his band, and as a schooled musician to whom the overall musical effect was vastly more important than showmanship. Another leader to instil into his performances a similar warmth and tonal richness was Ray Noble, the one Englishman to achieve equal fame on both sides of the Atlantic. A talented composer, Noble was also a master arranger who won a *Melody Maker* contest in 1926 at the age of nineteen and established himself in the profession with his scores for Jack Payne's BBC Dance Orchestra and its 1932 film *Say It With Music*.

Appointed as musical director to HMV Records in 1929, his recordings with the company's house band, made up of the finest musicians from London's top bands, made him one of the biggest names in British music, although he never actually led a working dance band there. Ray Noble's scoring has dated less than almost anyone else's and some of his ensemble effects have a marvellous sonority and depth. The band's repertoire was limited to the hits of the day, but one firm asset was the singing of Al Bowlly, the most individual band vocalist Britain ever had and who, like Noble, became equally popular in the States. I use the term 'band vocalist' advisedly, for in all his long career Bowlly seldom worked as a single act. From his first recordings, made in Berlin in 1927 with Arthur Briggs's Savoy Syncopators, Al Bowlly must have worked on more sessions than any other singer in the world; but although he was well-known enough from his regular employment with Roy Fox and Lew Stone it wasn't until something like a quarter of a century after his death in the London blitz of 1941 that he became a cult figure. Both EMI and Monmouth-Evergreen have reissued dozens of Noble-Bowlly recordings of the thirties and it may be difficult at this stage to decide whether Noble's arrangements or Al's singing are the selling point. Ray Noble's own attitude towards the whole thing was summed up quite succinctly when he told me in 1963:

> I feel myself that a new generation will not go for the nostalgia bit and will consider the records as merely rather dated. For years I kept a few scores for old times' sake and also to remind me how little I knew then and how lucky I was to have the whole-hearted enthusiasm of so many good musicians. Apart from that I would still like to have had the company consult me about the issue but no doubt they felt it wasn't necessary, especially as they don't have to pay me anything.

Noble's modesty apart, that last sentence is most revealing. For although the record reissues are labelled as by Ray Noble and his Orchestra they were originally made by the

New Mayfair Dance Orchestra with Noble, as arranger and conductor, working on a fixed scale as a record company employee. Whether the situation has now changed I have no means of knowing, as Noble remains incommunicado in his Jersey home. But isn't it ironic that, at least at that time, he was deriving no royalties from his revived and enduring fame as the leader of one of the greatest British bands?

In 1934 Ray Noble went to America, and for the first time worked in public as a bandleader in the Rainbow Room on the 65th floor of the RCA building in New York City. Glenn Miller, then trombonist and arranger with the Dorsey Brothers Orchestra, assembled a ready-made band for Noble to take over when he arrived accompanied by Al Bowlly and drummer Bill Harty. The band was a good one and some of the ballad arrangements have the warmth of the London recordings, but basically the problem was that Glenn Miller had formed the band, and in sharing the arranging with Noble was introducing a lot of his own ideas in the swing idiom. Sidemen like Charlie Spivak, Will Bradley and Claude Thornhill, embryo leaders themselves, Bud Freeman, George Van Eps, Pee Wee Irwin and Johnny Mince were rooted in swing era music; in fact Miller used most of the band in April 1935 for his first records under his own name. Faced with this dichotomy of ideas and styles it's hardly surprising that Ray Noble, feeling he could hardly call his band his own, left for Hollywood where he settled for further fame and security as musical director and comic stooge on the Edgar Bergen radio show, also appearing in a number of screen musicals. Thus, while Ray Noble's career in music, a distinguished one by any standards, spanned over thirty years, his honoured place in the world of big bands is assured by the sterling work he did in London's HMV studios from 1929–34. It is those records which, more than any others, exemplify the nostalgia which so many people have for this period.

Many other dance bands were active in the States during this era. Some of them, like Ted Lewis, Guy Lombardo, Ben Bernie, Jan Garber, Irving Aaronson's Commanders, Roger Wolfe Kahn and Mal Hallett, were bands which had started in the twenties or before but which really got into the swing of things in this, the heyday of dance music. Chicago, always a centre of big band music second only to New York, sported three eminent trumpet-playing leaders, Dick Jurgens at the Aragon and Trianon Ballrooms, Clyde McCoy at the Golden Terrace Cafe, and ex-Whiteman star Henry Busse at the Chez Paree. McCoy and Busse were basically good horn men who preferred to identify themselves with corny muted playing best expressed through their (self-written) signature tunes, Busse's 'Hot Lips' and McCoy's 'Sugar Blues'. Many of the bands were built round singing front men, few more eminent than film star Buddy Rogers. A musician before he was an actor, Rogers made his first film in 1925 at the age of twenty-one, and for some years combined the two careers. On trumpet and trombone he led his California Cavaliers at the Hotel Pennsylvania Roof, New York, including men like Gene Krupa, Johnny Mince, Mike Doty, Ward Silloway and Ray Biondi who went on into the ranks of the big swing bands. Buddy Rogers came to England in 1934 to make a film appropriately called *Dance Band*, recorded with top session men and conducted Jack Hylton's band on stage. Russ Columbo, who succeeded Bing Crosby as vocalist with the Gus Arnheim band at the Coconut Grove in Hollywood, also combined several careers, as violinist, actor, leader of a band which included Benny Goodman, Joe Sullivan and Gene Krupa, and as a singer whose popularity could have equalled that of Bing had he not died as a result of a tragic accident in 1934. Smith Ballew was notable only for leading a band that featured Glenn Miller, Ray McKinley and others who left to form the nucleus of the Dorsey Brothers Orchestra, though obviously without any hard feeling on the part of Ballew who featured as a rather mediocre vocalist on Miller's first recordings under his own name. Famous today as actor and comedy monologuist, Phil Harris started in the late twenties as drummer and co-leader of the Lofner-

Harris orchestra on the West Coast. Taking over the band as his own Harris featured himself and film starlet Leah Ray as singers and eventually found an outlet for his brash but likeable persona as conductor on the Jack Benny radio show. There were other singing leaders, like Dick Robertson, Ozzie Nelson (who married film star Harriett Hilliard, took his whole family and band into TV and radio, and unleashed his two sons, David and Ricky, on the world as pop singers) and Orrin Tucker, his own vocals taking second place to those of Bonnie Baker, whose hit version of 'Oh Johnny' took the band to the top in 1939.

So many bands one can't begin to list them all—Eddy Duchin, Matty Malneck, the Hudson-De Lange Orchestra, Dick Stabile, Richard Himber, Tommy Tucker, Del Courtney, all of them providing a training ground for musicians and singers who went on to the top bands. They made a good living and made millions of people happy for a while, and their names are only remembered in books like this. But once in a while a name does recur in surprising circumstances. Like Ted Weems, who led an entertaining band based on vocal novelties like the whistling solos of Elmo Tanner. In 1933 Weems and Tanner recorded a novelty shuffle rhythm version of 'Heartaches' to which the publishers, Leeds Music, and writers Al Hoffman and John Klenner objected so strongly that the disc received no exploitation and Guy Lombardo picked up all the sales. Fourteen years later a disc jockey in North Carolina found a copy and began playing it. It was reissued and sold a million, giving a new lease of life to Weems who, after two decades of only moderate record sales, got yet another Gold Disc the same year (1947) for 'Mickey'. It was a better outfit than the novelty angle might suggest, and was quite strong in the vocal department, for in the mid thirties Weems's boy and girl singers were a couple of promising youngsters named Perry Como and Marilyn Maxwell. Many men found bandleading a stepping stone to other things, and these are dealt with elsewhere, but this is the right context in which to mention Mitchell Ayres and his Fashions In Music, formed by violinist Ayres with some of his colleagues in the disbanded orchestra of 'Little' Jack Little. Though they worked good hotels for many years and appeared in films with the Andrews Sisters, Mitch Ayres only really came into prominence after World War II as Columbia's recording supervisor and Perry Como's television conductor.

On the whole, American thirties' bands of the non-swing variety aren't much of a talking point, but two of those offering a superior type of big band music verging on the swing style are worth a special mention. Hal Kemp is one of those legendary figures more heard of than heard. He was no stranger to London in his early years, first visiting as a nineteen year old college band leader in 1924 and returning in 1930 for dates at the London Coliseum and Café de Paris with a band that included jazz trumpeter Bunny Berigan. Midway through the decade the Kemp orchestra, through the arrangements of John Scott Trotter, developed the style that made it one of the most individual of bands. The trademark was staccato, triple-tonguing brass phrases against unison clarinets, supported by a smooth, danceable rhythm. When the band pulled the stops out as in 'Dodging A Divorcee' or 'Serenade For A Wealthy Widow' it made an impressive ensemble sound, brass and saxes blending in rich-sounding block chords. The star personality was Skinnay Ennis, a long, lean drummer with a breathless way of singing songs like 'Got A Date With An Angel' (the band's theme) that matched the orchestral style perfectly. But when Ennis left to take over the band on Bob Hope's radio show, and Trotter also left in 1936 to become Bing Crosby's musical director, the band lost its identity and Kemp entered the swing band stakes, incidentally with Janet Blair as vocalist. How it would have made out we'll never know. Driving between one night stands in December 1940 Kemp was killed in a car crash in California. Singer Bob Allen tried to keep the band going, then Art Jarrett, but to no avail. Few Kemp recordings are available, but in the early seventies John Scott Trotter led a session band in a delightful recreation of the Hal Kemp hits, but for me the unison vocal quartet just couldn't make up for Skinnay Ennis's absence. He had died ten years previously. Although the Kemp style died in America it was adopted in Britain by both Geraldo and Billy Ternent. The former's flirtation with brass triple-tonguing was short-lived compared with Ternent's whole-hearted adoption of it, which he still uses today along with the lush (some say schmaltzy) ensemble sound of saxes and brass. Jan Savitt's Top Hatters also perched midway between sweet and swing, their trademark being a shuffle rhythm characterising both ballad and up tempo numbers. Savitt, a Russian immigrant whose father was a drummer in the Czar's Imperial Regimental Band, was something of a prodigy, leader of the Savitt String Quartet and Stokowski's concert master while in his mid-teens. The Top Hatters came into being on Philadelphia radio and were soon touring and playing the top hotels, featuring the singing of George Tunnell (Bon Bon). Savitt, too, engaged a girl singer who left him for a film career, and Gloria De Haven's expertise in many MGM musicals is probably due to the experience gained by working with a top band. Another, sadder analogy with Hal Kemp is that Savitt also died

Jan Savitt, master of the 'shuffle rhythm' featured by his Top Hatters. (*RCA Records, New York*)

Lew Stone, the quiet pianist-arranger who became a leader under protest and created one of the finest British bands of all time. (*Mrs Joyce Stone*)

travelling between one nighters in California, being stricken with a cerebral haemorrhage in 1948, at the age of thirty-nine.

To say that the early thirties were peak years for British bands is to understate the case. Some were pretty awful of course, and even the best of them were subject to commercial considerations in choice of material. Yet more British than American dance music of this period has survived, thanks to enthusiasts within record companies with access to vintage recordings, to societies, clubs and magazines devoted to bands and singers of the 78rpm era, but, most of all, to men like Ray Noble, Lew Stone, Ambrose, Roy Fox, Henry Hall, Jack Hylton, Carroll Gibbons and all the others who created a form of music which, although inescapably of its period and therefore 'dated' in a sense, is still valid today. Without doubt the most influential figure in British music was Lew Stone (if this seems to conflict with my comments on Ray Noble, I am referring to Lew Stone as a working rather than a studio bandleader). This influence was not limited to his own great band, as before he formed it in 1932 his arranging had formulated the style of the Ambrose orchestra between 1927 and 1931. In great demand as a freelance, Lew's first scoring was done while he was pianist with Bert Ralton's Savoy Havana Band; he arranged and played piano on Sophie Tucker's double-sided record of 'My Yiddishe Momma', and his charts were used on many Columbia and Imperial records by the bands of Jay Whidden, Debroy Somers, the Starita brothers Rudy, Ray and Al, Jack Payne and Percival Mackey *et al.* It was as pianist-arranger with Roy Fox at the Monseigneur Restaurant that Stone first

Lew Stone and his Orchestra with Al Bowlly at the microphone. Some of the famous Stone sidemen include Nat Gonella (trumpet, 3rd from r), Bill Harty (drums), Joe Crossman (clarinet), Joe Ferrie (trombone, 2nd from r), Tiny Winters (bass), Alfie Noakes (trumpet, r). (*Mrs Joyce Stone*)

emerged from the back room, and when Fox was hospitalised for eight months in 1932 Lew took over the direction of the orchestra. Upon Fox's return the management asked Stone to continue as leader, and when Roy Fox went to the Café Anglais with a completely new personnel his old band, including Nat Gonella, Joe Crossman, Tiny Winters, Joe Ferrie and Al Bowlly, carried on as the Lew Stone orchestra.

The precision and swing of the Lew Stone band set a standard unique in West End dance music, and the national exposure it received via regular weekly broadcasts, prolific recordings for EMI and Decca, and stage appearances throughout the country, created a reputation that endures today. When Bowlly headed Stateside with Ray Noble he was replaced by Alan Kane, who maintained a high standard of singing on ballads. Obviously the band's location in a plush West End spot, plus the commercial schedule imposed on it by record companies, allowed little scope for jazz or swing, but occasional showcases like 'White Jazz', which it played every bit as well as the Casa Loma Orchestra, showed its potential. Lew Stone's own feeling for jazz was confirmed in the early days of the war when the draft and economic conditions compelled him to front a small group, the Stonecrackers, which gave some admirable jazz performances. Meanwhile Roy Fox, a Californian who had played trumpet with Art Hickman and Abe Lyman, found equal success at the Café Anglais and the Kit Cat Club, where his new band became as great a favourite with dancers and radio listeners as his Monseigneur band had been. It could swing when required but the Fox band was best in quality ballads, melodic with a good ensemble sound, sweet but never sugary, with vocals by one of the few good British singers. Denny Dennis was billed as 'The English Bing Crosby' which probably hindered his chance of ever becoming a big solo name, though in the postwar years he did sing with Tommy Dorsey's band for a year or so. Quite frankly, the general standard of band vocalists in the thirties was abysmally low, in America as well as in Britain, and for me at least it's the spineless, weak and watery singing, completely lacking in character, tonal quality or even the most rudimentary sense of phrasing or interpretation, that mars so many vintage recordings. It's easy to see why the term 'crooner' fell into such ill repute and equally hard to imagine how such appalling performances ever came to be regarded as the norm. No names, but few of them outlived the era, understandably so. Mind you, there are a handful of British singers who still sound good and, as well as Al Bowlly and Denny Dennis, I can listen quite happily even now to old recordings by Sam Browne and Alan Kane, both of whom were featured with the Ambrose Orchestra in the thirties.

Bert Ambrose was one of those legendary characters whose story could fill a book alone, but it's enough for us that he led one of the finest bands of all time. Unlike Lew Stone, the creative leader par excellence, Ambrose neither composed nor arranged, and his musical talent was limited to routine fiddle playing. A popular society figure but never merely a front man, he was a band *leader* in every sense who hired the best talent and knew how to use it, a disciplinarian whose musicians seldom took him seriously so unorthodox were his methods of imposing his will. Alan Kane, who must have sung with more bands than Al Bowlly, tells of an example:

On one occasion I was singing with a floor full of dancers, and I suppose it was an off night for me, when I had a tendency to sing flat, one thing Ambrose would not tolerate. He stood next to me and played the melody on his violin, but played it slightly sharp and grimaced with a sour look on his face to demonstrate his agony. I took the hint and it was a good lesson for the future.

This discipline, however applied, made for a tremendous rapport between leader and men, as on another occasion related by Alan—a Christmas night broadcast in 1938—when an eminent tenor, unused to dance band work, was guest artist:

He anticipated his cue and came in two bars early. With millions of listeners tuned in to this Christmas show Ambrose, demonstrating his supreme authority and control, hushed the orchestra to fade out, signalled the pianist to jump two bars and catch up with the singer in the verse, bringing the full orchestra in at the chorus to build to a wonderful climax.

Bert Ambrose, a Londoner born in 1897, started playing in a New York cinema, and in 1917 was musical director at the Palais Royal, NY, returning in 1922 to conduct at the Clover Gardens. This served him well for his famous residencies at the Embassy Club and the Mayfair Hotel, where he built an all-star band, the impact of which was first felt in the mid-twenties, and by the time 'Ammie' started his weekly broadcasts from the Embassy Club in 1933 he was in an unassailable position in the business. With a powerful outfit that included the great trombone trio of Lew Davis, Ted Heath and Tony Thorpe, Max Goldberg as lead trumpet, the singing duo of Sam Browne and Elsie Carlisle, and drummer Max Bacon, the rotund, bald Jewish comic who was nevertheless regarded by Gene Krupa as one of the world's great drummers, the quality of the Ambrose orchestra was founded initially on Lew Stone's arrangements, and latterly on the work as composer and arranger of baritone sax-clarinet player Sid Phillips. Ambrose returned to the Mayfair in 1936, and during the war, although suffering from the same draft problems as other leaders he continued to record for Decca featuring Anne Shelton, the finest girl singer Britain ever produced, a youngster with a marvellously mature vocal quality and a musicianly approach to good songs. In the fifties Ambrose recorded for MGM with a large concert orchestra scored (and possibly conducted) by Laurie Johnson whose arrangements, though obviously inspired by Robert Farnon, proved a good grounding for his later work in films and TV and with his own orchestra. The last time I saw Ambrose he was leading a nondescript little band at the Café de Paris around 1956, and he later went into artists management until his death in 1971.

Almost side by side in London's Park Lane, the Dorchester Hotel and Grosvenor House were palaces of high living outside the reach of Joe Public yet familiar to millions of radio listeners through the regular broadcasts of Jack Jackson and Sydney Lipton. Jackson,

Ambrose and his Orchestra. A hallowed name in British dance music, in whose ranks could be seen saxophonists Sid Phillips, Joe Crossman and Danny Polo, the famous trombone trio of Ted Heath, Lew Davis and Tony Thorpe, drummer-comedian Max Bacon, Max Goldberg (trumpet) and Reg Pursglove (violin); (Inset) **Bert Ambrose** himself (*2nd from left*) with three of his star singers **Anne Shelton** (*right*) **Vera Lynn** (*left*) and **Alan Kane** (*2nd from right*). (*EMI Records; Polydor Records; Alan Kane*)

former lead trumpet with Bert Ralton, Jack Hylton, Ambrose, Fred Elizalde, Percival Mackey, Jack Payne and others, was a natural leader with a happy personality (which stood him in good stead in the late forties when he became one of Britain's leading disc jockeys) and as good a jazz style as any British musician of the time. His band did little that was memorable but reissues remind us that it was capable of good dance music, stylishly arranged and played, with vocals by Sam Costa, Denny Dennis, Alberta Hunter and, on occasion, Al Bowlly. Sydney Lipton had the archetypal West End hotel band, but the expert musicianship of sidemen like George Evans, Ted Heath, Jock Cummings, Archie Craig, Harry Hayes and Bill McGuffie throughout the years ensured that it was one of the best of its type. A recently heard interpretation of one of Raymond Scott's involved pieces suggests that Lipton's was a very competent band indeed with the right material.

The last of the Big Six with a regular radio showcase was Harry Roy, a frenetic showman who introduced himself, after the theme music of 'Bugle Call Rag' as 'Your little hot-cha-cha'. His leadership and singing on swing numbers and novelties were obviously in emulation of Cab Calloway, but when he played clarinet and sang on ballads what came out was second-rate Ted Lewis, which makes listening to some of his old records something of an embarrassment. Much of the band's material was jazz-based and arranger George Scott-Wood had a flair for things like 'Tiger Rag', 'Temptation Rag', 'Casa Loma Stomp',

Jack Jackson blows a Bix-influenced obbligato behind **Fred Latham's** vocal chorus. (*World Records*)

Celia Lipton sings with father **Sidney Lipton and his Orchestra** at the Grosvenor House Hotel (Ted Heath is the one-man trombone section). (*Memory Lane*)

'Canadian Capers' etc. Unfortunately anything arranger and band did was negated by the ubiquitous two-piano team of Ivor Moreton and Dave Kaye, the Tiger Ragamuffins. Moreton and Bill Currie sang, but the best of Harry Roy is represented by the performances recorded minus vocals and pianos. Then it's easy to see why the listening millions and the patrons of the Café Anglais and the Mayfair Hotel gave Harry Roy his place in the dance music hierarchy.

Radio made these bands, and many others. The BBC had a policy in the 1930s of presenting live broadcasts from these West End haunts every night of the week, each band having its own regular night. But the BBC has always promoted dance music, and from the early days of radio until the present time has sponsored its own dance orchestra. The first

On stage during a frenetic moment in a **Harry Roy** performance at the Pavilion Theatre, Piccadilly, in 1937; (Inset) drummer **Joe Daniels** and 'The Tiger Ragamuffins', **Ivor Moreton and Dave Kaye,** featured musicians in the Roy Band for many years. (*Alan Kane; EMI Records*)

An audience-eye view of a typical **Jack Payne** stage show of the thirties with Billy Scott-Coomber at the microphone. (Note the six saxophones at a time when three were the norm).

was Sidney Firman's London Radio Dance Band, which broadcast from the original BBC studio in Savoy Hill in 1926. This nine-piece included in its ranks saxophonist Jack Padbury who was to lead his own band, and banjoist Pasquale Troise, whose Mandoliers were great light music favourites in later years. The first actual BBC Dance Orchestra, formed in 1928, was directed by Jack Payne, band leader from the Hotel Cecil. Payne's programmes covered the whole musical spectrum, but he specialised in comedy numbers and semi-legitimate concert pieces. One of my own memories (I was only about nine or ten at the time) is of Payne's breathless announcements including (heaven knows why I should remember this, but it's one of those silly things that sticks in the mind) one of 'a concert transcription of "Trees" '. Like his contemporary Jack Hylton, Payne was influenced by

Henry Hall. (*Henry Hall*)

Paul Whiteman, but lacking Whiteman's jazz flair his own work often sounded ponderous. When he left in 1932 for stage work (see Chapter 6) it became the BBC Dance Orchestra directed by Henry Hall, from the new corporation headquarters in Broadcasting House, the start of an association that endured via the popular *Henry Hall's Guest Night* series long after he ceased leading a regular band.

The Hall orchestra was always tasteful, and his employment of American jazzman Benny Carter to contribute arrangements was a highlight of British dance music, not least for the fact that Carter's presence in England in 1936 led to a number of interesting recording sessions under his own name featuring the cream of London jazz musicians. Henry Hall had a variety of vocalists, the first being Val Rosing, who typified everything that was wrong with band singers of the times. His successor was a Canadian sax player, Les Allen, who had come to Britain with Hal Swain's New Princes Toronto Band in 1925, and whose good looks and pleasant style endeared him to listeners. Dan Donovan, Bob Mallin, successive drummers Len Bermon and George Elrick, both of whom did comedy vocals, and glamorous blonde Phyllis Robbins (always much too coy for my taste) helped make Henry Hall the biggest radio favourite of them all.

At the outbreak of war the BBC moved its Variety Department to Bristol and gave the leadership of the Dance Orchestra to former Jack Hylton deputy leader-arranger Billy Ternent. The orchestra was more of a utility unit accompanying all types of programmes, but Ternent was given individual air time for his Sweet Rhythm, the style based on Hal Kemp's, which even in those days was beautifully nostalgic in sweet music style, and remains even more so today. Ivy Benson and her All Girls Band, although not classed as the BBC Dance Orchestra, received an official appointment during the war, and in 1944 Stanley Black took over the officially titled band. Still on general utility lines, this did feature Black's own style, a more sophisticated approach than Ternent's, rooted in his own wide background (playing piano on Coleman Hawkins records at twenty, and with top bands like Ambrose, Harry Roy, Lew Stone and Maurice Winnick). Twenty years later Stanley Black was conducting the London Philharmonic but his tenure with the BBC remains a landmark in both his career and the corporation's existence.

In 1952 they changed the name to the BBC Show Band and gave the baton to Cyril Stapleton, who twenty years before had been a nineteen year old violinist in Henry Hall's BBC Dance Orchestra. Demobbed from the RAF Symphony Orchestra after the war, Stapleton had organised a very neat little band for Fischer's Restaurant, consisting of one trumpet (Tony Osborne) and five saxes scored in Glenn Miller style. The Show Band was given peak listening time in its own show, often with guest stars of the calibre of Frank Sinatra and Tony Martin, and Bill McGuffie had a weekly solo spot which established him as Britain's greatest pianist in either jazz or melodic style. The Stapleton band may have lost some of its individuality in growing to mammoth proportions, but it remained a first-

Brought to London by ex-Art Hickman saxophonist Bert Ralton for a 1922 Coliseum engagement, **The New York Havana Band** went on to the Savoy Hotel to become the first Savoy Havana Band. (*Savoy Hotel*)

class orchestra by any standards. In Manchester the BBC formed its Northern Dance Orchestra, an offshoot of the Northern Variety Orchestra, which conductor-arranger Alyn Ainsworth turned into a first rate swing band presented in admirable style on radio and TV by the subtle humour of compère Roger Moffatt. Later taken over by Bernard Herrmann (not the film composer) the NDO has latterly continued to present the best in big band music, along with the London-based Radio Big Band. Although for a decade or so the BBC has been largely pop-orientated, it still obviously retains a soft spot for the dance music traditions it started nearly fifty years ago. It may have taken us off course and away from the Golden Years for a page or two but the BBC's sponsorship of big band music is perennial and cannot be overlooked in any history of British dance music.

Nor can one overlook the importance of London's Savoy Hotel as a source of outside broadcasts, a residency for the cream of dance bands and a meeting ground for the best

American and British musicians in those halcyon years when all the American big bands visited London and locals and visitors could work side by side. It was a state of affairs that became impossible a few years later when Musicians' Union problems caused a complete ban on the appearance of American musicians and bands in Britain, but at the outset the Savoy's musical policy was based on imported bands. Joe Wilbur and the Savoy Quartet started it all in 1916–19 followed by Bert Ralton's New York Havana Band from 1920–3. There was a short visit by Frank Guarente's Georgians in 1923, following which Reg Batten took over the Savoy Havana Band from 1923–7 (one of the saxophonists was Rudy Vallee, who wasn't considered good enough to sing with the band). At this time the stand was shared by Debroy Somers and the Savoy Orpheans, and when Somers left in 1926 to form his own band the Orpheans were led briefly by Cyril Ramon Newton, Carroll Gibbons taking over from 1927–8. Fred Elizalde and his Music were there during 1928–9, being replaced by Al Collins and Geraldo and his Gaucho Tango Orchestra in 1930. Carroll Gibbons returned from Hollywood where he had been working with MGM, and remained at the Savoy from 1931 until his death in 1954. Canadian Billy Bissett guested during 1936–7, ex-Squadronaires leader Jimmy Miller was there after the war, Roberto Inglez led the Latin-American band during the fifties, and after Gibbons's death the Savoy's music was, as it still is, in the hands of Ian Stewart. A confused genealogy perhaps, but it shows that the management actively encouraged a solid musical policy and that for several decades the name of the Savoy was synonymous with the best in dance music.

Perhaps it was this same hidebound conservatism that precluded universal acceptance of coloured leaders like Rudolph Dunbar and Reginald Foresythe who attempted to inculcate new and colourful ideas into routine British music. Dunbar had studied music at Columbia University and played in the pit band of the Broadway show *From Dixie To*

The most memorable Savoy maestros of the earlier years were Debroy Somers and Fred Elizalde, two men whose music and personalities couldn't have been more disparate. Somers, tall and distinguished, conducting in morning suit or tails, was the epitome of the

Carroll Gibbons and the Savoy Hotel Orpheans. Back row (l to r): Max Abrams, Jack Evetts, Ian Stewart, Carroll Gibbons, Bert Thomas; centre: Bill Shakespeare, Billy Higgs, Arthur Fenhoulet, Paul Fenhoulet, Sam Acres; front row: Reg Leopold, Eugene Pini, Laurie Payne, George Melachrino, George Smith, Bob Wise. (*Savoy Hotel*)

correct Englishman. His music, including the Savoy Medleys which were in the library of every semi-pro band in the thirties and forties, was equally British accented, correct, precise and purely functional. Elizalde, on the other hand, was an imaginative Spanish-American who gave the Savoy patrons undiluted jazz. His band included Adrian Rollini and other members of the California Ramblers, and though short-lived is still an unforgettable part of British jazz history, although it does seem to have suffered, both in its recordings and its hotel work, from the inability of the British public to accept revolutionary musical ideas and the inevitable need to compromise between commerce and art.

Perhaps it was this same hidebound conservatism that precluded universal acceptance of coloured leaders like Rudolph Dunbar and Reginald Foresythe who attempted to inculcate new and colourful ideas into routine British music. Dunbar had studied music at Columbia University and played in the pit band of the Broadway show *From Dixie To*

Reginald Foresythe's New Music produced some of the more 'progressive' sounds of the thirties, including his famous compositions 'Serenade For a Wealthy Widow' and 'Dodging a Divorcee'. (*World Records*)

Debroy Somers and his Orchestra in a British film of the thirties. (*Gainsborough Pictures*)

Broadway before going to Paris for further clarinet studies. He played in *Blackbirds* at the London Pavilion in 1926, gave solo recitals and finally became a bandleader, appearing at the Prince's Restaurant with his African Polyphony. Little was heard of him in later years until his name became accepted in classical music circles as instrumentalist and composer. Reginald Foresythe was a British citizen of German-West African parentage who had played piano with Paul Howard's Quality Serenaders in California while writing for films in Hollywood. He wrote Earl Hines's theme 'Deep Forest' in Chicago en route back to London where he formed his New Music, a nine-piece that played at the Café de la Paix and 400 Club. Foresythe's New Music was an all-reed combination which he used to experiment with new ideas of composition, and listening to such pieces as 'Dodging A Divorcee', 'Berceuse For An Unwanted Child' and 'Serenade For A Wealthy Widow' the similarity between Foresythe's creations and those of Raymond Scott a few years later is not limited to a predilection for odd titles.

   Like Dunbar, Ken 'Snakehips' Johnson came from British Guiana and presented an all-coloured band at the Florida Club. Although none of its records have been available for many years, my memory tells me that Johnson was unique in playing big band music that effected an expert compromise between its inherent swing style and the commercial demands of the music business. The most banal tunes came over with a verve that compensated for occasional ensemble roughness, and Johnson's death in an air raid on the Café de Paris in 1941 before he became wider known was a sad loss to the profession. Heaven knows there were few enough swing bands in Britain at the time. Elsewhere I mention Nat Gonella and his Georgians, George Scott Wood and his Six Swingers and Joe Daniels and his Hot Shots. Playing the same sort of arranged 'hot' music were Claude Bampton and his Bandits—he later fronted a band of blind musicians with George Shearing on piano and Carlo Krahmer on drums—and George Elrick and his Swing Band. Freddy Gardner, mainstay of the Ray Noble orchestra and probably the country's finest altoist, put together a combination for a Rex Records session in 1938 that showed how good a British big band could be even with commercial material. A long-gone name that evokes a sense of nostalgia is that of Teddy Joyce, a tall, personable Canadian violinist-dancer-compère and ex-conductor at Warners' Hollywood theatre who fronted an all girls band in 1938 (a twenty-four piece with Ivy Benson on lead alto), sponsored a boys band in 1935, led his own big band in films and on stage (once with Joe Venuti at the London Palladium) and in 1935 opened his own Continental Club with a sixteen-piece band that featured such jazz stars and session men of the future as Harry Latham, George Chisholm, Duncan Whyte, Jimmy Macaffer, Robert Busby, Andy McDevitt *et al.*

As in America, so many bands. Studio bands of arrangers like Percival Mackey, Jay Wilbur, Harry Leader, Phil Cardew, Van Phillips, Phil Green, Harry Bidgood; run-of-the-mill dance bands of no particular significance like Jan Ralfini, Howard Jacobs, Arthur Roseberry, Herman Darewski and many others—all helping to make the prewar years indeed the Golden Age Of Dance Bands. Not all of them survived the era, or even the decade, for in the forties dance music was to undergo a metamorphosis as complete as that at the end of the twenties. It was in the Golden Age, however, that two of the most durable bandleaders of all first made the big-time at the Astoria Ballroom in London's Charing Cross Road. Billy Cotton had his first band in the Royal Flying Corps during World War I, in which he served as a teenage pilot. He played drums in other groups after the war and finally became a professional leader at Ealing Palais de Danse in 1921, working his way round the provinces until his 1928 West End debut at the Astoria proved a stepping stone to Ciro's Club. Strange though it may seem to those who know Cotton only as a somewhat corny showman, his early work, with a band that included at various times Sydney Lipton, Nat Gonella and his brother Bruts, Teddy Foster, Joe Ferrie and Sid Buckman, was considered quite 'hot' for the times, recording as many jazz standards as pops. He even gave his bands such evocative names as the London Savannah Band and the Cotton Pickers, a common practice among British bands, maybe in the belief that you can fool some of the people some of the time? Two years after Cotton's debut at the Astoria the same stand was occupied by a nine piece fronted by twenty year old Joe Loss, a former cinema violinist who had learned to cater for dancers at the Wimbledon Palais, and whose experience at the Astoria led him to the Kit-Cat Club. By 1935 the Loss band had grown to four brass, three saxes and four rhythm, but like Billy Cotton the young leader didn't care much for society work, finding more affinity with the ballroom crowds—so back to the Astoria. Chick Henderson, the singer responsible for the Loss hit record of 'Begin The Beguine', was killed on active service during the war, by which time Loss was playing for war-weary dancers, entertaining servicemen and topping the bill in music hall. His other star vocalist reflected an ephemeral trend of using 'straight' singers in a big band context. This was dark and swarthy, romantic singer Monte Rey, clad in exotic Latin costumes, who sang exotic Latin songs in an enormous non-rhythmical voice. The fiery Latin was actually a mild mannered, middle-aged Scotsman named James Montgomery Fyfe, but that's show business! One of the few bands still going, Joe Loss's hold on the public over forty-five years cannot be denied. Musically the band has never been either impressive or original, always holding a mirror up to the latest American trends and reflecting them back to a public that prefers the home-made, however derivative, to the real thing. Why else would Joe Loss's biggest record hits be Miller's 'In The Mood', Herman's 'Woodchoppers Ball' and a quite fantastic album seller in the seventies devoted to carbon copies of Glenn Miller hits?

Imitative or not, though, the fact that records of such uncompromising swing music could become best-sellers in a country not previously renowned for any mass interest in jazz or swing was a pointer to the direction in which big band music was going. Had been going for quite a while, in fact, for by this time the Swing Era in America was at its peak.

3 THE SWING ERA THE BIG BIG BANDS

More nonsense has been written about the Swing Era than any other period in the history of our music. On the one hand there was contempt from jazz purists, criticism by society dancers, and sociological comment from people in general on the bobbysoxers and jitterbugs who gave swing music its biggest public. (Those same bobbysoxers, the 'rebels' against parental authority, are now the 'square' parents who are themselves victims of the present generation's rebellion against conformity just as their own parents were the equally rebellious and shocking gay young things of the twenties—so what else is new?) At the other extreme there is the overdone nostalgia bit, the deification of Glenn Miller, the archetypal figure of the Swing Era.

But time has a remarkably mellowing effect as well as enabling the onlooker to view things in the right perspective. So, with the swing bands all but a memory, the erstwhile purists now find them a surprisingly fruitful field for research, though is it really surprising when you consider that virtually every jazz man of eminence played in the big bands at some time or other? Record companies on the other hand regard the Swing Era as a perennial source of income from both reissues of original recordings and stereo remakes by studio bands of the vintage scores of Miller, Dorsey, James *et al*. The former can be a source of frustration, the latter one of annoyance—frustration with companies which sit on valuable and seldom-heard masters or adopt a policy of endless reissues of over-familiar material; annoyance that a great deal of money and time is spent in endless recreations of a few dozen popular but hackneyed themes, recordings which, however well done, are still mere copies of something that was done, and done better, thirty years ago. The whole point about the music of the Swing Era, its *raison d'être*, is that the bands, each of them with its own individual style, played their own music written especially for them with their own ensembles and soloists in mind. Duke Ellington, to quote the prime example, wrote his whole library to suit not only his featured soloists but the whole texture of the orchestra as it was at one specific time with the musicians who gave it that tone. Just one instance. When Cootie Williams left the band 'Concerto For Cootie' was dropped from the repertoire (it became the song 'Do Nothing Till You Hear From Me'). It was Williams's vehicle, written for him. Nobody else could play it. Hence Ellington's ever-changing repertoire, for unlike other leaders he seldom rested on his laurels. A moment had come and gone, another moment was at hand. If I want to listen to swing music I play Woody Herman's 'Caldonia', Bob Crosby's 'South Rampart Street Parade', Bunny Berigan's 'I Can't Get Started', Jimmie Lunceford's 'For Dancers Only' or Tommy Dorsey's 'Well Git It'. It's not simply that these bands played them better than anyone else. These records encapsulate a moment in time, the act of creation. Anything else, however brilliant a contemporary recreation from session men in deliberately nostalgic sessions by Glen Gray and a late fifties phoney 'Casa Loma Orchestra', Enoch Light and the Light Brigade, Syd Lawrence or the Time-Life series of remakes, remains just a copy. How *could* we expect an ad hoc band in one session to adopt the identities of a dozen long gone bands each with its own style, sound and voicings?

The most vital aspect of the Swing Era, and the real difference between swing and dance music, was that the bands were led by musicians many of whom were also composers and arrangers who could either create or dictate a personal style, and who were capable of literally leading their bands on their own instruments. It was Harry James as lead trumpet who gave his brass section its own tone, and can one begin to imagine the orchestras of

Titular leader of the co-operative Casa Loma Orchestra in its palmy days,
Glen Gray returned in the late fifties to revive his own and other Swing
Era hits with an orchestra of top session men.

Duke Ellington. (*Pye Records*)

Benny Goodman, Artie Shaw, Tommy and Jimmy Dorsey, Lionel Hampton or Charlie
Barnet without the leaders' own contributions? Previously so many bandleaders had been
business men, mediocre musicians (if they played at all) or 'front men' with no musical
knowledge but a flair for smooth liaison between band and public. The Swing Era was
responsible for so many talented bandleaders who had risen from the ranks and were able
to communicate with their sidemen on a level footing.

The dominant figure of the Swing Era—let's amend that: the predominant big band
figure of the last fifty years—was Edward Kennedy 'Duke' Ellington, the supreme creator
of orchestral jazz, of whom it has often been said that his instrument was the whole
orchestra. From the first 1925 recordings with his Washingtonians to his death in 1974 as
a spry seventy-five year old he never let up for a day, taking his orchestra round the world,
playing one of the most individual and I think underrated pianos in jazz, and creating—
always creating. The measure of Ellington's particular genius is that so many of his pieces
which passed into big band history were less the result of burning the midnight oil over
piano and manuscript paper than of ideas being tossed around in the studio as 'head'
arrangements, emerging after a couple of run-throughs as perfectly formed master works,
classics in miniature. The Count Basie band worked on the same principle but there's a
world of difference between Basie's riff themes and Ellington's beautifully crafted compositions. Not all the Ducal works happened this way, naturally, but it is a fact that some
of those now-famous records were only given titles long after the session, and sometimes
the Duke himself didn't really know what he had recorded. (One suspects in this the
fine hand of music publisher Irving Mills, who handled Ellington's music for many years
and also managed to cut himself in as lyricist or even 'co-composer' on dozens of the most
valuable Ellington properties.)

The empathy between Duke Ellington and his colleagues is evident in the long service
of men like Johnny Hodges, Sonny Greer, Barney Bigard, Paul Gonsalves, Jimmy Hamilton
and, especially, Harry Carney whose tenure with the band lasted nearly half a century.
Although the style varied superficially over the years, Duke always managed a perfect compromise between the fundamental Ellington sound and the fashions of the moment. The
1940-2 edition with Ben Webster and Jimmy Blanton is generally regarded as his finest
band, and certainly the seventy-two records it cut for RCA Victor during that period
represent his zenith of creativity and performance, revealing in such pieces as 'Cottontail',

Ben Pollack, whose prolific recording activities in the twenties and thirties provided Goodman, Miller, Teagarden, Spivak, James and other future band leaders with some of their earliest experience as sidemen. (*Universal-International Films*)

Between 1930 and 1947 **Mills Blue Rhythm Band** operated under a variety of leaders and pseudonyms. **Lucky Millinder** conducts the 1934 version which later carried on under his own name. Musicians include trumpeter Henry 'Red' Allen Jnr (between bass and drums), Buster Bailey (clarinet), J. C. Higginbotham (trombone next to guitar), Joe Garland (tenor), Edgar Hayes (piano).

'Harlem Air Shaft' and 'Never No Lament' a complete mastery of the three-minute form. But then the Brunswicks of the thirties ('Echoes Of Harlem', 'Diminuendo and Crescendo In Blue', 'I Let A Song Go Out Of My Heart'), the 1946 Musicrafts ('Sultry Sunset', 'Beautiful Indians'), the 1947–50 Columbias culminating in 'The Hawk Talks' (possibly the least typical Ellington number ever but a superb example of big band swing) —any of these are also peak periods. Duke Ellington it was who, having mastered the three-minute form, first extended jazz beyond those confines with 'Black Brown And Beige', the delightful 'Perfume Suite' and other longer works right up to the full-scale religious compositions performed shortly before his death.

The early careers of Ellington, Fletcher Henderson, Don Redman and Benny Carter are closely intertwined, with appearances on each other's recording sessions and exchanging of arrangements. Although Henderson's scores for the first Benny Goodman band were responsible for the Swing Era itself, his own early band was served mainly by the arrangements of alto sax Don Redman, who left him in 1927–8 to assume leadership of a corn band founded by drummer William McKinney. Redman's writing and direction soon had McKinney's Cotton Pickers rated as one of the finest of the early swing bands, before he left in 1931 to take over Horace Henderson's band under his own name. Redman's career at this point closely paralleled that of Benny Carter, who had played with Ellington briefly before joining Fletcher Henderson as alto sax and arranger. He took over McKinney's Cotton Pickers from Redman before also leaving to form his own band. Incidentally, there just isn't room in a book of this size, attempting to cover a fifty-year span, to go into the ramifications of the recording industry and its pseudonymous bands; the sort of process by which both Don Redman and Fletcher Henderson recorded as 'Connie's Inn Orchestra',

Count Basie and his Orchestra (Jo Jones, Walter Page, Buddy Tate, Freddie Green, Buck Clayton, Dickie Wells), in a New York jam session in 1940. (*Jazz Monthly*)

or by which the 'Chocolate Dandies' was actually at various times a label name for the orchestras of King Oliver, Benny Carter, Buster Bailey, Don Redman and Mills Blue Rhythm Band. This latter, known originally as the Cocoanut Grove Orchestra before the ubiquitous Irving Mills tacked his name on to it, also recorded as Mills Music Makers, King Carter and his Royal Orchestra, Earl Jackson's Musical Champions, Harlem Hot Shots, Duke Williams and his Orchestra, and Earl Harlan and his Band, as well as working under the names of its successive leaders Baron Lee and Lucky Millinder. That sort of confusion is meat and drink to jazz researchers but life's too short. This is why I haven't gone at length into the studio set-ups of Ed Kirkeby, Ben Pollack, Sam Lanin, Red Nichols and other recording directors who functioned under different names whenever they entered a recording studio.

These early coloured swing bands played music in which the traditional New Orleans style of jazz was either forsaken or developed by skilled arrangers into an orchestrated form of jazz generally referred to as 'hot'. A surprising source for bands of this ilk was Kansas City, from whence came Harlan Leonard, Alphonso Trent, Jay McShann, Andy Kirk's Twelve Clouds Of Joy, Walter Page's Blue Devils and Bennie Moten, whose band was taken over on his death by William 'Count' Basie, its pianist. Kansas City style was based on the riff motif in which repeated rhythmic phrases are used either thematically or behind soloists, and Basie was supreme at this technique in those early days—'One O'Clock Jump', 'Swinging The Blues', 'In The Mood' and 'At The Woodchoppers Ball' are prime examples of riff pieces.

One of the most prominent showman-leaders was Cab Calloway, even though his title of 'Prince Of Hi-De-Ho', and his antics and frenetic singing, tended to obscure the many fine musicians who found security in the highly paid ranks of the Calloway band. But to give him credit, Calloway realised that he himself sold the band to a mass public as a showcase that would be good for talented musicians, and he did whenever possible give space to soloists of the calibre of Ben Webster, Doc Cheatham, Chu Berry, Jonah Jones, Hilton Jefferson *et al*. Dizzy Gillespie was in the band in 1940–1, and though Cab Calloway told me a decade or more later that Diz and other kindred spirits were a great trial to him, his former pianist Benny Payne told me a few months afterwards that Calloway was a good boss, with more forbearance than many would have had. Calloway was actually an excellent singer when not clowning, and when I interviewed him in 1952 was starring as Sportin' Life in the world tour of *Porgy and Bess*. He had succeeded Duke Ellington at the Cotton Club in 1931 and was himself followed in 1934 by Jimmie Lunceford, with one of the most powerful and influential big bands of the thirties, due to the arrangements of Sy Oliver, Lunceford's no-nonsense direction, and a sense of showmanship that made the band as great a visual attraction as it was on radio and records. All that business with sections standing for climaxes, trumpets pointing skywards and trombones circling the clock—all the things that Glenn Miller and a dozen others did—Lunceford did first. Nor was this the only influence exerted by the Lunceford band. When Sy Oliver went over to Tommy Dorsey in 1939 he obviously made the influence felt in his own scoring, but this apart one can sense an appreciation of the Lunceford spirit—that easy mid-tempo at which the band was so great, the solid ensemble punch and the sheer swing of the whole band— in the scores Billy May did for Glenn Miller and his own band of the fifties, in the pile-driving riffing ensembles of the Lionel Hampton band, in the whole concept of the later Basie band. It appears in a big band LP of 'Romantic Jazz' by Jackie Gleason in the late fifties which Oliver arranged and conducted. When Lunceford died in 1947 the band died with him. Physically, that is. In every other way its memory and influence are undying.

Cab Calloway and his Orchestra, one of the more obviously commercial coloured bands, but some good jazz could be heard behind Cabell's extrovert posturing and 'Hi-de-hi-de-ho' vocals.

The saxophone section of the 1946 **Jimmie Lunceford Orchestra** (l to r) William Horner, Omer Simeon, Kurt Bradford, Joe Thomas, Earl Carruthers, with Fernando Arbello (trombone) far right and Charlie Stewart just visible on trumpet.

Chick Webb died young in 1939. He was thirty, a hunch-backed dwarf who led from behind his drums what must have been the most swinging band of all. Much of this comes across on records in Edgar Sampson's clean-limbed scores, but from all accounts the band in person at the Savoy Ballroom in Harlem had to be heard to be believed. Other great bands would come into the Savoy for a cutting contest, as they were called, and every time the Webb crew would blow the visitors right off the stand. Yet Chick Webb was best known to the public for his sponsorship of the sixteen year old singer his front man Bardu Ali discovered in an amateur contest at the Apollo Theatre in Harlem. He took Ella Fitzgerald into the band in 1934, and Chick and Mrs Webb adopted the young orphan. Her vocals, musicianly then as now, were an integral part of the band's repertoire; but it was the 1938 hit record of 'A-Tisket A-Tasket' that was the turning point for Ella. She had fronted units from the main band on records as Ella Fitzgerald and her Savoy Eight, but it was that big hit that gave her the standing in the profession to be able to take over the orchestra as her own when Webb's spinal disease proved fatal. With Teddy McRae and Eddie Barefield as musical directors, Ella kept the band going until 1941–2 when the ever-increasing demands on her time as a soloist forced her to disband.

Teddy Hill's band visited the Savoy on many occasions while Webb was resident, but although he featured such star jazzmen as Chu Berry, Roy Eldridge, Dickie Wells and Russell Procope, Hill was neglected by record companies, making but a couple of dozen sides for Vocalion and Bluebird, none of which have been available for years. Apart from his 1937 employment of Dizzy Gillespie, Hill contributed notably to the bebop movement of the early forties when he retired from bandleading and opened Minton's Playhouse, the night club in which Gillespie, Charlie Parker, Kenny Clarke, Thelonious Monk and the other begetters of bebop began their musical experiments.

Claude Hopkins and Edgar Hayes were other big band leaders of note playing primarily to black audiences at venues like the Savoy, as was Erskine Hawkins, who came to New York with his 'Bama State Collegians in 1936 and also recorded, though more prolifically than Hill, for Vocalion and Bluebird. Not at all well represented on record in Britain at least, the Hawkins band had two semi-hit records by which it's best remembered, the catchy 'Tippin' In' and pianist Avery Parrish's blues feature 'After Hours'. It could be rough at times, but the band is in retrospect perhaps one of the most typical examples of the second-string coloured bands of the period.

We seem to have come a long way along the road of jazz and swing without mentioning the most outstanding jazz musician of all. For although Louis Armstrong will be remembered most for the Hot Fives and Sevens of the twenties and the All-Stars in the postwar years, he writes his own chapter in the history of big bands. He led one for nearly twenty years on stage, radio and ballroom dais but it was seldom his own. Satchmo borrowed other people's bands like another trumpeter would borrow mutes, and when (if) he gave them back they were never quite the same again. First of all, in 1928–9 he used fiddler Carroll Dickerson's band as his own, then the Cocoanut Grove Orchestra-cum-Blue Rhythm Band. Louis Armstrong's Sebastian New Cotton Club Orchestra of 1930 was actually Les Hite's orchestra with Lawrence Brown, Marshall Royal and seventeen year

Luis Russell and his Saratoga Club Orchestra c. 1930. Led by Russell on piano, the personnel includes Henry 'Red' Allen Jnr (far r), J. C. Higginbotham (3rd from r), Pops Foster (4th from r), Paul Barbarin (7th from r), Albert Nicholas (8th from r)

old Lionel Hampton, but most of the time between 1929 and 1941 he fronted Luis Russell's orchestra, recording now and again with the Dorsey Brothers Orchestra, the Casa Loma Orchestra (once, even, with Andy Iona and his Islanders!). He also led a medium-sized band of mixed lineage in Paris in 1934 but, like every big band Louis ever had, its role was clearly defined—to support Louis and nothing else. Satchmo took the trumpet out of the New Orleans ensemble and gave it a virtuoso voice in jazz, never more so than when fronting his own band (his predilection for Lombardo-ish saxophones was notorious and this in itself would be enough to write most Armstrong bands off as swing units). None of the early Armstrong orchestras was worth a dime as a band, but a seventeen piece he had in 1946-7, while it wouldn't have won any cutting contests with Herman or Gillespie, made pleasant commercial dance band noises even when Louis was not soloing.

All the bands mentioned hitherto were coloured and however commercial their operation they were still rooted in jazz, or at least the basic principles of jazz as applied to orchestrated music. White bands had contributed little to date except for the star-studded Paul Whiteman and Jean Goldkette orchestras, which were hardly swing bands as such. Goldkette had by this time settled in Detroit supplying bands for various functions, including a group called The Orange Blossoms which, by 1929, included trombonist Pee Wee Hunt, saxist Glen Gray and guitarist Gene Gifford, also a very talented composer and arranger. This band was to play at a new club called the Casa Loma, in Toronto, and though the place never did open the band adopted the name and set up as a cooperative unit. After prestige locations like New York's Roseland Ballroom and the Glen Island Casino, the Casa Loma Orchestra clinched its success on radio for Camel Cigarettes (for which its famous theme song, Gifford's 'Smoke Rings', was so appropriate), the first time a swing band had been on a sponsored programme. Now fronted by Glen Gray, an impressive six and a half footer, it was the first white swing band to compete with the coloured bands, a comparison ironically pointed by Gifford's best known pieces 'White Jazz' and 'Black Jazz'. The Casa Loma lacked the essential free-wheeling spirit of its mentors, but technically it played admirably and paved the way for the deluge of white bands which followed. Originally Gene Gifford was the presiding genius, a fine writer whose influence on swing as a whole should not be under-estimated. His place was taken in 1935 by Larry Clinton from the Dorsey Brothers Orchestra, but two years later Clinton himself left to form his own band which he used as a vehicle for his composing and arranging. The Clinton band recorded prolifically for Bluebird but little of its output has survived and Clinton himself is best remembered for his songs 'My Reverie' (via Debussy), 'Dipsy Doodle' and catchy instrumentals like 'Study In Brown' and 'Spooky Takes A Holiday'.

The year 1935 was a turning point for many people. Charlie Barnet had been leading a fairly successful band since 1933; the Glenn Miller/Ray Noble band had just made its mark; Ben Pollack's band had just reformed under Bob Crosby; Isham Jones's band was about to do the same under Woody Herman, and the Dorsey Brothers Orchestra was about to blow up in a welter of brotherly recriminations. But still it was all just dance music and 'swing' was a verb rather than a noun. Then Benny Goodman emerged as 'King of Swing' and things were never the same again. What brought about the cataclysmic upheaval was the demise of the Fletcher Henderson orchestra, the leader presenting many of his own scores to Benny Goodman. The twenty-six year old Chicagoan had been leading studio groups since 1928, generally composed of the familiar New York faces who did sessions with Red Nichols and Ben Pollack, with whom Goodman had started his career in 1926. He formed his first regular band in 1934, but his name meant so little to the public that one of his records was issued under the name of Harry Rosenthal's Orchestra in America and The Broadway Bandits in Britain! With such Henderson scores as 'King Porter Stomp' and 'Sometimes I'm Happy' the new Goodman band proved a hit on the *Let's Dance* coast-to-coast radio show, and after six months Goodman took to the road expecting to recreate his success in person. But a cross-country trek on one-nighters disillusioned him to the point of considering disbandment, until they hit the Palomar Ballroom in Los Angeles. There Benny found the audience he had been looking for and the kids found the kind of revolutionary music they wanted. From then on it all happened, climaxed by a stage show at the New York Paramount that had them literally dancing in the aisles. Swing was the thing and Goodman was the King, jitterbugging became a national pastime, bobbysoxers were invented and a whole new impetus was given to big band music.

Goodman was unfairly criticised by the jazz purists who considered his band less righteous than Fletcher Henderson's, which had used the same arrangements more authentically without the fame and fortune. In fact, most of the white bands came under fire as lacking the essential jazz feeling that informed bands such as Lunceford's, Basie's and Webb's. This may well be true, just as it's true that Goodman, Shaw, Miller and others, in playing to a predominantly white market, were receiving greater exposure and achieving record sales of astronomical figures while coloured bands were in many cases limited to the 'race' audiences and record lists. But then the American population was predominantly white, so is it surprising that sheer weight of numbers favoured them? Musically the white bands were polished to an unprecedented degree of sophistication, but they were basically dance bands rather than jazz outfits and it would be ostrich-like to pretend that they didn't swing at all.

It was Goodman's initial success that sparked off the personality cult, in which a band's star sidemen received solo exposure and public acclaim in equal proportions. The fan worship accorded Harry James, Gene Krupa, Ziggy Elman and Lionel Hampton during their stay with B.G. encouraged them to form their own bands and assured them of a ready-made audience when they did. Not the least of Goodman's achievements was the formation of the band-within-a-band—the Goodman Trio, Quartet and eventually Sextet—which, with Teddy Wilson on piano, Lionel Hampton on vibes and Gene Krupa on drums, played a unique form of chamber jazz which will stand forever as a model of small group playing, with empathetic teamwork almost unparalleled in musical history. Benny Goodman also made history of a different nature, for his employment of black musicians like Wilson, Hampton, Cootie Williams, Fletcher Henderson, Charlie Christian, Slam Stewart and singers Ella Fitzgerald and Jimmy Rushing was instrumental in breaking down certain racial barriers.

In forty years Goodman seldom did the unexpected and has always retained not only the sound of the thirties band but many of the old Henderson and Edgar Sampson scores. After the war he flirted with bop unsuccessfully, and only once was the Goodman band in any sense progressive. In 1939 he switched record companies from RCA to Columbia; Helen Forrest and, later, Peggy Lee, took over the vocal spot held by Helen Ward, Louise Tobin and Martha Tilton and, most important, he signed Eddie Sauter as arranger. Sauter, ever a tasteful and wonderfully imaginative writer, changed the band's image completely, rejecting the old brass against saxes formula in favour of more harmonically advanced scores on ballads, some of which presaged the great sounds of the Sauter-Finegan Orchestra a decade later, and ingeniously crafted originals such as 'Clarinet A La King' and 'Benny Rides Again'.

I'm not entering any arguments about whether Goodman or Artie Shaw was 'King of the Clarinet', though Shaw used the title. Maybe B.G. had a little more jazz feeling and the technique that enabled him to play chamber music and classical concertos with the world's leading orchestras. But Shaw was his equal in front of a big band, while his playing in the

Mel Tormé, singer-composer-arranger-actor-author-vocal group leader; quite a talent, but he started as a teenage drummer with a band led by Chico Marx, before making big band history with his Meltones on Artie Shaw's 1946 Musicraft recordings. (*Polydor Records*)

Artie Shaw. (*RCA Records, New York*) **Jimmy Dorsey**

smaller context of his Gramercy Five or the string group with which he first appeared, is noted for its subtlety and delicacy. Shaw, the most outspoken of men, sounded off at various times about jitterbugs and all the aspects of the business which displeased him, and was constantly retiring in disgust. But he always came back with something new. His original New Music, recorded on Brunswick in 1937, was the nearest he came to having an uncompromising jazz band, but the even newer 'new music' assembled in mid-1938 which got its sendoff with 'Begin The Beguine' was the equal of any swing band of the time. This hit record was the work of Jerry Gray, who had been with Shaw right from the start as violinist and arranger, and when Gray went over to Glenn Miller in came a young trombonist and arranger named Ray Conniff from Teddy Powell's band. Shaw delighted in good standards and show tunes, and the string-laden orchestra of 1940–1 produced some of the most stylish and tasteful dance music ever recorded. During the war Chief Petty Officer Shaw led an all-star navy band that played for servicemen all over the Pacific, and when he was discharged on health grounds it carried on under Sam Donahue and Claude Thornhill. The band he put together on his return in 1944 was a more modern crew spotlighting the trumpet of Roy Eldridge and some swinging scores by Conniff, but the most impressive Shaw records were a set of Cole Porter tunes he did for Musicraft in 1946 with a forty-piece orchestra and some of the finest vocal group singing of all time from twenty year old Mel Tormé and the Mel-Tones, whose 'What Is This Thing Called Love?' is a musical milestone. In later years Artie Shaw attempted several comebacks, but finally passed out of the business completely to make a new name for himself as an author.

Like Goodman and Shaw, Jimmy and Tommy Dorsey came out of the New York studios, but the Pennsylvania Irishmen had first played in the Paul Whiteman orchestra of 1927 after making a purely local reputation with their Scranton Sirens. After years of sessions for Ben Pollack and Red Nichols, the Dorsey Brothers studio orchestra became a working dance band in 1934 with Glenn Miller as trombone/arranger, Ray McKinley on drums and vocals by Bob Crosby and Kay Weber. But the brothers, brilliant musicians and forceful personalities, were incompatible as co-leaders and the inevitable break-up was sparked by a trivial incident—an argument about the tempo of 'I'll Never Say Never Again Again' one night in 1935 at Glen Island Casino. Tommy walked out and took over the nucleus of the Joe Haymes band while Jimmy kept the Dorsey Brothers band as his own. The split was fortuitous as well as inevitable, for in going their separate ways Jimmy and Tommy Dorsey gave the world two of its finest dance orchestras, each fired by the talent and temperament of its leader. Jimmy was more commercial, making his name with such forties ballads as 'Tangerine', 'Amapola' and 'Green Eyes' featuring the sweet and swing vocals of Bob

In later years it would have cost any promoter a fortune to engage the **Tommy Dorsey** orchestra with (l to r) singers **Frank Sinatra** and **Jo Stafford,** trumpeter **Ziggy Elman** and drummer **Buddy Rich.** In 1941 the entire package was available for Union scale, one of the few bands in which the vocals were no anticlimax. (*RCA Records, New York; Universal-International Films; Gramophone Record Review*)

Eberly and Helen O'Connell, but on the right day his band could swing with the best of them on up-tempo things like 'John Silver' and 'Grand Central Getaway'. For me there's nothing more evocative than Jimmy's rather old-fashioned but adroit and highly individual alto noodling in front of the ensemble. Unless it's Tommy Dorsey's smooth and gentle trombone, on which his superb control and phrasing and tone made him the envy of every trombonist in the world and earned him the title of 'The Sentimental Gentleman of Swing'. Jimmy's band may have had dull patches when the material wasn't inspired but I don't think Tommy ever had a band that was less than perfect, even his most commercial records possessing a style that is still irresistible.

At first Tommy's style was formulated by arrangers Paul Weston, Axel Stordahl and Deane Kincaide, Sy Oliver and Bill Finegan later joining the team to create a more advanced style befitting the larger band of the forties. Prewar singers Edythe Wright and Jack Leonard were replaced in the forties by Frank Sinatra, Connie Haines, Jo Stafford, Dick Haymes, The Pied Pipers and Stuart Foster, and with this impressive sequence of future stars Tommy Dorsey's was about the only band in which the vocals didn't come as an anticlimax. RCA's release, in the early seventies, of a boxed set containing all eighty-three titles that Sinatra recorded with Dorsey shows that these pop tunes were turned out to a seldom varying formula—opening chorus from the Tommy Dorsey trombone, Sinatra vocal, rhythmic band chorus and out—but it was a pleasant style that could benefit the most banal song. Plus, of course, the already marvellously mature voice of the greatest pop singer of all. At up tempos the Dorsey crew swung mightily, fed from behind by Buddy Rich's drumming and inspired by the trumpet solos of Bunny Berigan, Max Kaminsky, Ziggy Elman and Yank Lawson. In the boom days of 1942–5 Dorsey was one of several leaders to add strings, and while Artie Shaw used them as a section phrasing with brass and saxes to create an integral effect, even on rhythm tunes, Dorsey used his almost symphonically to create a mood. 'Opus One' and 'On The Sunny Side Of The Street', two of T.D.'s most famous records (with Nelson Riddle on second trombone, did you know?), show how Sy Oliver used the strings at jazz tempi in a purely sustaining role. From the start of the Swing Era and 'Song Of India' through to the fifties Tommy Dorsey went his own way, neither setting nor following trends, and even when that distinctive trombone was tacit the band was always identifiable by that superior musicianship on which this doughty taskmaster always insisted.

In the early fifties the brothers came together again and the sound of the Dorsey Brothers Orchestra was once more heard in the land, playing the old hits of both leaders and a new book of ballads scored for a big, lush ensemble, plus some effective swingers from Basie arranger Ernie Wilkins. The battling brothers had belied their tempestuous exteriors by making some of the most beautiful of all popular music. They couldn't work together for long, but they couldn't live without each other, and when Tommy died in his sleep in 1956 Jimmy was heartbroken, and only six months later himself succumbed to the cancer he never knew he had. Ironically, he died a few days after receiving a Gold Disc for his 'So Rare', one of the few big band records to make it big in the fifties.

In the mid-thirties, before it went shooting off at tangents, jazz was still rooted in Dixieland and the blues with boogie as an offshoot, and some white swing bands did a more than passable job of interpreting these idioms in big band style. Outstanding both commercially and artistically was the Bob Crosby Orchestra, which came into being when Ben Pollack's big band broke up in 1934. The musicians stayed together on a co-operative basis under saxist Gil Rodin's leadership, hiring Bob Crosby as front man. A fair singer overshadowed by big brother Bing, Crosby was the only swing band leader who was neither a musician nor musical director of his own band. Although a mere figurehead Bob was respected by his men for his lack of any pretensions about his own talent and importance and, more particularly, for his love of the band's music. Scores by Deane Kincaide, Matty Matlock and Bob Haggart combined the spirit of New Orleans jazz with the sound of the Swing Era, and the big band arrangements of jazz standards plus Haggart originals like 'South Rampart Street Parade' made a truly joyous noise, while the Bobcats, the band-within-a-band, produced some of the best small group Dixieland of the decade. With Yank Lawson, Eddie Miller, Ray Bauduc, Joe Sullivan, Irving Fazola, Jess Stacey and other star jazzmen who also had the facility and temperament for big band work, the jazz feeling was on a par with the musicianship. Others who were later destined for big things passed through the Crosby band, and many years later Bob Crosby told writer George Simon how he tried and turned down singers Johnny Desmond, Doris Day, Gloria De Haven and Kay Starr. Said Crosby, 'Come to think of it, we fired some pretty great arrangers too, like Ray Conniff, Henry Mancini, Nelson Riddle and Paul Weston!'

Excellent though the Bob Crosby Orchestra was at big band Dixieland I think Muggsy Spanier's big band of the early forties was even better. Deane Kincaide also scored for this band which seemed more vital and exciting than Crosby's, but unfortunately was much less durable, due to Spanier's less tractable attitude towards the commercialism necessary to maintain a big band economically, and his inability to keep a stellar personnel. So it's Bob Crosby we remember, and Spanier's finest memorial remains the 1938 RCA Victor jazz sessions. 'The Band That Plays The Blues' was the tag attached to Woody Herman a decade or so before the First Herd blew the Swing Era into orbit with its high-flying arrangements. Saxophonist and singer with the Isham Jones Orchestra, Woodrow Wilson Herman had learned his craft in the bands of Tom Gerun (he shared sax and vocal duties with Tony Martin, and boy-and-girl duets with Ginny Simms), Harry Sosnik and Gus Arnheim. On Isham Jones's retirement in 1936 the key members of the band stayed together on a co-operative basis with Herman as titular leader and Gordon Jenkins, Joe Bishop and Chick Reeves writing the book. The Herman band's blues and boogie recordings may have been commercially slanted but they played them with reasonable conviction, coasting along for three years until Bishop's 'At The Woodchoppers Ball' gave them the open sesame to the big dates and more hit records. Though they later dropped the blues angle and played swing and dance music with equal conviction and flair, Herman's was never really one of the swing idols prior to its metamorphosis in 1945, dealt with in the next chapter. Jay McShann combined blues and boogie with his own energetic Kansas City style, and his band of the early forties has a place in the history books for giving Charlie Parker his earliest record exposure a few years before he and Dizzy Gillespie revolutionised jazz with bebop. At the riff game Count Basie was supreme, although when critic John Hammond first persuaded MCA to bring the band in from Chicago it was far from the great outfit it eventually became. But despite rough spots its enthusiasm and excitement were infectious, and it improved enormously during its first Manhattan engagement at the Famous Door with soloists like Lester Young, Buck Clayton, Harry Edison and blues singer Jimmy Rushing, all of whom were as vital to the band as the arrangements which, like 'Doggin' Around', 'One O'Clock Jump', and 'Jumpin' At The Woodside', were basically simple riffs, more or less improvised. Members of the band contributed scores, but basically it was this seemingly spontaneous combination of joyful solos springing from equally enthusiastic ensembles that made such a contrast to the more facile and sophisticated routines of the white swing bands.

Boogie had always been a basic jazz piano idiom, but for a time in the early forties it became widely popular in big band form, largely due to the efforts of Will Bradley and Freddie Slack. Bradley, a studio trombonist who had played in the Ray Noble/Glenn Miller band as Wilbur Schwichtenburg, teamed up with pianist Slack and drummer Ray McKinley in a band that, whatever else it may have played, is best remembered for boogie novelties like 'Down The Road Apiece' and 'Beat Me Daddy Eight To The Bar' featuring McKinley's oddball vocals and Slack's righteous piano. But as had happened with the Dorseys, and Noble and Miller, it proved impracticable to have a band with two leaders, and after Slack capitalised on his fame by starting his own band in 1941 McKinley and Bradley split, the former to join Major Glenn Miller's Army Air Force Band, the latter returning to studio work. Freddie Slack's share of the boogie market was assured with his 'Cow Cow Boogie' record hit of 1943, which helped put the new Capital Records company on the map and established the career of singer Ella Mae Morse. But although he did well enough Slack never reached the upper echelon of big bands, a common fate of many talented sidemen who lacked the flair for showmanship and business which was an essential prerequisite of the successful bandleader. Why else should superb musicians like Bunny Berigan and Jack Teagarden have failed in front of their own big bands? Too easy-going, perhaps, in a cut-throat business where leaders had to be as tough with their musicians as with managements and agencies? Both were fine, dedicated musicians (Berigan is only one contender for the trumpet crown, but few, if any, trombonists could begin to compare with Big T.'s warmth, genuine jazz feeling and instrumental technique) who were at their

Bunny Berigan who never did get started commercially, but made his own niche in jazz history as a sideman and soloist.

best when relieved of responsibilities and playing for other people. Berigan has been the subject of almost as much sentimental legend as Bix Beiderbecke, including the inevitable application of the title of his best-known record 'I Can't Get Started' to his own life, and like Bix he destroyed himself in the end. His band, in which Ray Conniff, Georgie Auld and Buddy Rich cut their teeth musically speaking, was good, but Berigan is best remembered for his solo contributions to Goodman and Tommy Dorsey records. Jack Teagarden endured the trials of big band leading in 1939–40 in partnership with lead trumpet Charlie Spivak, and featuring singers Kitty Kallen and David Allyn, but the amiable Texan was less temperamentally suited to leadership and eventually returned to the more congenial world of small jazz groups and his long postwar stretch with the Louis Armstrong All Stars. Coleman Hawkins, the greatest tenor sax in jazz, was also essentially a soloist who flirted briefly with the big band idiom in 1940, using a fifteen piece on four fine sides for Okeh records, and pianist Teddy Wilson left Goodman about the same time to field an eleven piece featuring Ben Webster, but here again the ventures were shortlived.

On the other hand there's Benny Carter, one of music's really great all-round talents who knew orchestral technique inside out, always had good bands, yet was rarely as successful as he should have been. Maybe Carter was essentially a back room boy, a creator rather than a performer (as a leader, that is—as a musician he is one of the three greatest alto players of all time and a more than useful trumpeter). Whatever the answer, the handful of Benny Carter Orchestras that existed from 1933 to the mid-forties made some of the nicest music in the whole world of big bands. Carter was a unique composer and arranger, inventive and original with a true mastery of the orchestra, writing clear-cut lines for brass and saxes that must have been a joy to play. As already narrated, his first band was McKinney's Cotton Pickers, following his work with Duke Ellington, Fletcher Henderson and Chick Webb. The first under his own name came along in 1933 with Wilbur De Paris, Sid Catlett, Chu Berry, J. C. Higginbotham etc. Invited to London to arrange for Henry Hall's BBC Dance Orchestra, Carter made a number of records with top West End musicians of the calibre of Ted Heath, George Evans, Max Goldberg, Lew Davis, Freddy Gardner and Buddy Featherstonhaugh, before going on to the continent where he organised recording dates with the bands of Thore Ehrling in Stockholm, Kai Ewans in Copenhagen, Coleman Hawkins, The Ramblers and a mixed British-European-American band in Amsterdam, and a Franco-American group with Django Reinhardt in Paris. Back in New York in 1939 he formed a band for the Savoy Ballroom, disbanded, reformed in late 1940 for the Famous Door, and finally left for Hollywood where he settled down, alternating between studio work and fronting night club bands with freelancers like J. J. Johnson, Neal Hefti, Bart Varsalona, Shorty Rogers, Emmett Berry, Trummy Young, Flip Phillips *et al*. Benny Carter was thus unique in being the first coloured leader to break down more racial barriers by fronting a mixed band, by his employment as Mark Warnow's arranger on radio's *Your Hit Parade* and, more importantly, in the Hollywood film studios where he scored and appeared in such films as *Thousands Cheer, An American In Paris* and *Snows Of Kilimanjaro*.

This is a good point at which to mention a British contributor to the swing era in the person of Patrick 'Spike' Hughes, sometime bass player and writer who was never a working bandleader but who organised a number of studio sessions between 1930–2 with British musicians and also used Benny Carter's 1933 band to interpret his own compositions. Hughes later became a journalist and author and developed more interest in classical music, but the few records he made over forty years ago are now collectors' items.

One of the last great coloured bands of the Swing Era to be mentioned was resident at the Grand Terrace Café in Chicago for most of the twenties and thirties under the direction

Earl 'Fatha' Hines, a great influence on jazz piano and a prominent big band figure in the transition from swing to bop. (*Jazz Monthly*)

of Earl Hines, the most influential of all jazz pianists since his recordings with Louis Armstrong's Hot Five and Seven. Hines kept a big band intact until the mid-forties but was better known to the jazz cognoscenti than the wider public until the inevitable record hit. The first was Hines's 1940 'Boogie Woogie On St Louis Blues', the second the 1942 'Stormy Monday Blues' featuring vocalist Billy Eckstine. Eckstine brought Dizzy Gillespie and Charlie Parker into the Hines ranks along with singer-pianist Sarah Vaughan, and for a while Hines had the first bop band, but as this happened during the 1943 AFM recording ban its reputation is confined to those lucky enough to hear it in person. Lionel Hampton turned up in the early forties with a big big band after organising all-star recording groups for RCA Victor between his dates with the Benny Goodman Quartet. A very technical if

Leader of a wild and sometimes rough big band, **Lionel Hampton** is himself one of the most musicianly and tasteful of soloists. (*Polydor Records*)

not always swinging drummer, a 'unique' pianist who used two fingers in the upper register of the keyboard like vibraphone mallets, and the world's greatest, most melodic, tasteful, inventive and swinging vibes player, Hamp never had the best band in the world, but it didn't matter. He sold excitement plus! Riffing, screaming, pounding, frantic exuberance that sounded thrilling enough on disc and must have been hypnotic to experience in person. For a soloist of such impeccable good taste in his own playing it was strange that this was not always reflected in the band, in which the ten brass and five saxes wouldn't necessarily be playing quite together! When he first appeared in London in 1956 Hampton was greeted by unprecedented fan fever, at a time when the Big Band Era was supposed to be over and the Rock Era starting. The raucous combination of blues, bop, rock and extrovert showmanship inspired one British bandleader to stand up and shout, 'Why don't you play some jazz?' But Hampton did. Not the cerebral jazz of Ellington, not the well-staged jazz of Lunceford, nor the melodic jazz of Carter, but its own we're-having-a-ball-and-this-is-where-it's-at kind of jazz. And if the players themselves are so involved that they

Charlie Barnet.
(*Polydor Records*)

Gene Krupa

get carried away by it then that *is* jazz! The close contest between Goodman and Shaw is nothing to that between Hampton and Kenneth 'Red' Norvo. No other vibraphone players come into it. It was a number of years before Norvo turned to the electrical instrument from the more orthodox xylophone, but such was his skill that the xylophone sounded less like a novelty instrument than it had done in the hands of vaudeville performers like Teddy Brown. Norvo's band of 1936–42 never attained the heights of other swing bands, though no less outstanding musically due to the subtle scoring of Eddie Sauter and the singing of Mildred Bailey (Mrs Norvo at the time). A rotund, inelegant lady, Mildred Bailey had a small, true, sweet and wonderfully rhythmic voice which blended well with the orchestra, but it was a combination less extrovert than Fitzgerald and Webb and there was no 'A-Tisket A-Tasket' to open doors. Norvo eventually replaced Hampton in the 1944 Goodman Quintet and was on hand in the 1946 Woody Herman band, his finest work being done in the Woodchoppers splinter group's wonderful small band sides 'Pam', 'Four Men On A Horse', 'Steps' etc.

Charlie Barnet and his Orchestra followed a familiar pattern of success, from its formation in 1933 (Eddie Sauter was in there too) enjoying moderate fame until the height of the Swing Era when he too had the record hit that turned the scales for him. This was Billy May's impelling arrangement of 'Cherokee', formerly a Ray Noble ballad. An unashamed Ellington disciple, Barnet entered a new milieu of hard-driving swing music with the help of May, a good hot trumpeter as well as a vital writer. With Lena Horne and, later, Kay Starr as vocalists, Barnet had a band that combined mass appeal with the respect of swing fans, and although he went through the forties with frequent personnel changes his output was remarkably consistent. Charlie Barnet didn't conform to the usual rags-to-riches story. His was a riches-to-riches background and he believed in work being fun, but he was never merely a dilettante and in retrospect was a more important contributor to the Swing Era than he may have seemed at the time.

I have already mentioned the Benny Goodman band's role as a training ground for future bandleaders, and it was inevitable that his two star soloists of the thirties, the sidemen who were as important to the fans as B.G. himself, should branch out on their own. Gene Krupa, showman drummer supreme, was a natural. He started the vogue for long, exhibitionistic drum solos complete with lighting effects, hair-tossing, gum-chewing —none of which meant a damn thing musically, except that Krupa happened to be one of the best drummers of all. Jazz buffs didn't (and don't) like him too much, but then they do tend to look at jazz through grey-coloured glasses. Although Krupa was the attraction he never hogged the limelight to the exclusion of his musicians. With men like Sam Donahue, Shorty Cherock, and Milt Raskin in the ranks and Roy Eldridge and Anita O'Day strongly featured, his band could well stand on its own. When he added strings and a touch of bop it was even better. 'Leave Us Leap' and 'What's This' showed that strings and jazz could go together, and when Gerry Mulligan started writing things like 'Disc Jockey Jump' after the war the band reached its peak. Thereafter Krupa, who had in later years fronted the band while Joe Dale played drums, returned to small group work, though he did revive some of his old scores with a pick-up band in the mid-fifties for Norman Granz's Verve label.

His former Goodman colleague Harry James never gave up. He put a band together in January 1939 and he still has it. He started out quietly enough with some good swing arrangements and nice singing from Frank Sinatra, whom he discovered working at the Rustic Cabin in New Jersey, but not much was happening professionally. Sinatra went over to Tommy Dorsey and was replaced by Dick Haymes and Helen Forrest, but until the combination of the leader's sweet trumpet and a small string section in 'You Made Me Love You' caught the public imagination the James band was still strictly for musicians. Harry James, a very fine jazz trumpeter, was caught between his natural desire to feature the best in swing music and the public's desire to hear more of that gorgeous open tone he displayed on ballads. Generally speaking he managed a first-class compromise, though his personal reputation among jazz fans suffered thereby. For twenty years the James band pursued its own course, uninfluenced by anyone. On the contrary, Harry James was himself an influence on Charlie Spivak, Sonny Dunham, Billy Butterfield and Randy Brooks, whose brazen, crystal clear horns in front of their own bands bespoke only too clearly James's own melodic style. Record hits, personal appearances, guest and starring

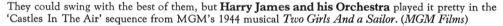

They could swing with the best of them, but **Harry James and his Orchestra** played it pretty in the 'Castles In The Air' sequence from MGM's 1944 musical *Two Girls And a Sailor*. (*MGM Films*)

Glenn Miller,
merely a success
in his lifetime, but
a legend and prime
influence more
than thirty years
after his death.
(*RCA Records,
New York*)

roles in films, even marriage to Betty Grable—James was the No 1 idol of the forties. A string section even larger than Dorsey's and Shaw's took some of the swing out of the band but created a beautifully luxurious mood on ballads. I heard the enormous orchestra many times at the Hotel Astor in New York in June 1945 and was more than impressed by the fine musical organisation it had become. It was no longer a jazz, or even a swing, band *per se*, but as a neo-symphonic dance band it had few equals. In the fifties the strings went out and, while there was still a compromise between sweet and swing, it was more the James band of old; but by the early sixties James finally severed all links with the past when Basie arranger Ernie Wilkins created a new look. Well, maybe not quite new. What came out was echt-Basie, but it was relieved from mere plagiarism by the solo work of veteran alto Willie Smith, the inspiring drumming of Buddy Rich and Harry James's own fluent lead that showed he hadn't forgotten a thing learned in the Goodman brass team a quarter of a century before.

Just one Swing Era name left, but it's one that means as much now as it did then. More, perhaps. How can you explain the perennial and enduring success of Glenn Miller, who died over thirty years ago but is still as much a part of the contemporary music scene in the seventies as he was at the height of his popularity? Why should RCA be reissuing every studio recording he ever made and seeking out old acetates of thirty-five year old airshots? What is there about the Miller sound that attracts fans to sell-out concerts of pseudo-Miller music? Why does a British fan spend thousands of pounds on a projected search of the English Channel for that tiny Norseman plane that took Major Glenn Miller to his death in wartime? True, he had a good band with an individual style and his records recall an era rich in nostalgia for those of us who were young then. But why not Shaw, James, Goodman, Dorsey or any other band that played the same things at the same time?

Intriguing questions. And I don't have a single answer. Despite many criticisms of the band—it didn't swing; it sacrificed feeling for mechanical perfection; it had bad singers—Glenn Miller remained the biggest draw in American ballrooms and theatres, on radio and jukeboxes. There have been and still are other bands playing Miller arrangements but without exception they achieved only the superficialities. Even Jerry Gray who helped create the original Miller band, and Tex Beneke who fronted the identical musicians after Miller's death, didn't make it. The inescapable fact is (a point I made in Chapter 2 re Isham Jones) that while Glenn Miller employed first-class musicians and writers, he was the catalyst who directed all these talents. A hard-driving man, a strict disciplinarian, it was the inspiration of Miller himself which welded all these diverse elements into the most popular and influential dance band in history. The fact that Miller played a fair ratio of swing arrangements, riff numbers, flagwavers and marvellously conceived orchestral works, didn't detract from the fact that this was a dance band whose reputation with the dancing public rested firmly on its performances of the hits of the day. And that was what Glenn Miller wanted. It was never his ambition to lead the world's greatest jazz band. Ray Eberly, Marion Hutton, Tex Beneke and the Modernaires were more important in the general scheme of things than Hal McIntyre, Ernie Caceres, Bobby Hackett, Billy May, Ray Anthony or any other of the fine musicians who filled the Miller chairs from time to time. He did sacrifice feeling for perfection. It was worth it—in dance band terms anyway.

There was far more to Miller's music than an easily identifiable (and God knows how imitable) saxophone sound. It was a trademark but never a formula. To accept the clarinet lead with tenor doubling as the be-all and end-all of Glenn Miller's music is to ignore the finer points of almost any score in the band's library. Even the most dedicated Miller fan can still listen to a favourite record and notice some felicity of scoring as though for the first time. Bill Finegan was the arranger most adept at that kind of subtlety, and while Jerry Gray's instrumentals best express what we now regard as the quintessential Miller sound we must never overlook the sometimes progressive and always exciting quality of Billy May's contributions to the library. Yet it can't be just that which attracts attention today. Claude Thornhill, Red Norvo, Boyd Raeburn and Duke Ellington were just as subtle if not more so. Lunceford, Hampton and Basie swung more. Dorsey and Shaw played equally pretty dance music. Yet Glenn Miller did all this in just four years. A business man whose business unwittingly became a musical legend, he would never have guessed that he alone would perpetuate the era of big bands not only twenty years after its demise but thirty years after his own.

4 THE END OF THE BEGINNING THE WAR YEARS

Dance and swing music received their greatest boost and achieved unprecedented popularity during the years of World War II, a period which actually overlaps what is generally regarded as the Swing Era but differs in so many essentials from the preceding decade that it deserves a chapter to itself. The progress of the top swing bands in the forties was discussed in the previous chapter, and they not only maintained but increased their popularity during those years when bright swinging music was the ideal panacea for what ailed the world. Theatres, ballrooms, radio and records provided relaxation for forces and civilians alike. In America defence workers and servicemen on furlough flocked to the big ballrooms from Roseland in the east to the Hollywood Palladium in the west, while in Britain, where the full impact of the war was felt at first hand, dancing was a relief from the more immediate tensions experienced by the civilian population. In America the major cinemas ran a feature film and a band show, and in Britain the big bands topped the bill in music hall at a time when every town of any size had its own variety theatre. In both countries and the principal theatres of war, dance bands joined the entertainers who embarked on ENSA and USO tours exclusively for the fighting men and women. The record industry, despite material shortages, had never known better times and independent companies proliferated, especially in the jazz and 'race music' fields. 1942 was a good year in which no fewer than thirteen band records sold a million copies each, although there wasn't really a swinger among them—Kay Kyser and Harry James in strictest ballad mood had four each for starters. All the top bands and singers embarked on a programme of recording special V-Discs for the armed forces, for which they all gave their services free. These records have since become collectors' items as many of the bands recorded material unavailable commercially.

During these years the old borderlines between sweet and swing tended to become rather blurred and even the 'mickey mouse' bands of Sammy Kaye, Jan Garber, Kay Kyser, Shep Fields and Horace Heidt began to jump. More to the point, as the draft played havoc with band personnel more sidemen found it an opportune time to go into business for themselves. The point has already been made that not all good musicians make good bandleaders, since only in very rare cases is the musical temperament—that wholehearted dedication to music essential to the man who wants to be more than just another musician—allied to

Even bandleaders took time out for socialising in those busy forties; (l to r) **Bobby Sherwood, Kay Kyser** and **Jan Garber.**

Remaining together as a unit after the war, the RAF No 1 Balloon Centre Dance Orchestra, known familiarly as **The Skyrockets,** are pictured at Hammersmith Palais in the days when leaders like Paul Fenhoulet still wore white tie and tails.

any sort of business sense. Plus the fact that many musicians are oddballs anyway and that the discipline necessary to control fifteen equally offbeat characters may well be missing from the embryo leader's makeup. Be that as it may, most of the new bands to emerge during the war years were the result of star sidemen branching out on their own, men like Roy Eldridge, Randy Brooks, Cootie Williams, Charlie Spivak, Gerald Wilson, Bobby Sherwood, Billy Butterfield, Sonny Dunham, Dizzy Gillespie (all trumpeters), Bobby Byrne, Georgie Auld, Hal McIntyre, Alvino Rey, Frankie Carle, Tony Pastor and Eddie Howard. They all gave up lucrative positions in top bands, and whether or not their ventures were to their financial benefit in the long run, each and every one enriched the scene in some way. There was no longer any arbitrary division between sweet and swing bands. They all played rhythmic dance music with a modern flavour, providing anything the customers wanted in the way of rhythm and/or romance. In a modern phrase, it was all happening, and only dear old Guy Lombardo and Wayne King never changed an iota. There were bands all over the place, even more than in the thirties. Even Chico Marx went out on the road with a band assembled by Ben Pollack and featuring Mel Tormé on drums.

Britain, ever the follower of America's lead, didn't start its own Swing Era till after the war, but even here big bands were getting bigger, and the four-man saxophone sections of the thirties gained depth and sonority as the addition of a baritone sax made the five-piece sax team the norm; too, the old three trumpet-two trombone brass sections grew into four of each. One of the inspirations for a renaissance of quality dance music in Britain was the formation of services bands which, subsidised by the armed forces for their own entertainment, were less subject to commercial dictates than the civilian bands, were independent of the whims of the public (they did after all have captive audiences), and being themselves draftees were assured of permanent personnel. The leading British bands were both Royal Air Force units staffed by eminent prewar musicians. The Squadronaires (the RAF No 1 Dance Orchestra) included many ex-Ambrose sidemen, while the Sky-rockets (the No 1 Balloon Centre Dance Orchestra) drew much of its personnel from Carroll Gibbons's Savoy Hotel Orpheans. The Squadronaires were then and are still, in retrospect, one of the finest bands ever known in Britain. Although based loosely on the Bob Crosby Orchestra, the Squads were a good all-round swing band—no, I'll rephrase that—they were a fine jazz band. They didn't have to please promoters or ballroom managers, and the jazzmen in the band like George Chisholm, Tommy McQuater, Andy McDevitt, Jock Cummings, Ronnie Aldrich, many of whom had made jazz/swing records before the war, played at their uninhibited best. It was with the Squadronaires that Chisholm, arguably Britain's greatest jazz musician, began to provide comedy relief, and

Former singer with Bob Crosby and Gene Krupa, **Johnny Desmond** established his postwar career through his fine work with Major Glenn Miller's American Army Air Force Orchestra.

it's a sad reflection on the importance of jazz to the British public that he is best known nowadays as a comedy trombonist. Sergeant Jimmy Miller fronted the Squadronaires, which were taken over after the war by pianist Ronnie Aldrich, but they became just one more band hustling a living, and although the musicianship was unimpaired the repertoire included too many references to Billy May, Kenton etc. The Skyrockets were directed during the war by Paul Fenhoulet, former trombonist with Percival Mackey, Jack Hylton and Carroll Gibbons. A less outstanding swing outfit, they were a useful all-purpose orchestra who continued after the war with Woolf Phillips as conductor and arranger. Their versatility stood them in good stead when Val Parnell picked the Skyrockets as house band for his London Palladium, supporting top American stars who found the band's modern style admirably suited to their more sophisticated orchestrations. The army and navy also had their bands, the Royal Army Ordnance Corps' Blue Rockets, led initially by Eric Robinson then by Eric Tann and Benny Daniels, and the Royal Navy's Blue Mariners under George Crow. These were less eminent as dance bands than as variety orchestras accompanying service and ex-service radio shows.

Then came the event that proved to have the most beneficial effect on British music—and the arrival on British soil of Major Glenn Miller and his American Army Air Force Band in June 1944 was certainly the greatest thing that had ever happened in my young life. This was no revamped version of the civilian Miller band but a whole new conception of big band music, and to those of us who listened avidly to its wartime broadcasts those were glorious musical days indeed. The Miller crew was on the air several times each week, both the full forty-one piece orchestra and the various sections which had their own programmes—Mel Powell's Uptown Hall Gang, Ray McKinley's Swing Shift, George Ockner's Strings With Wings and Johnny Desmond's Soldier With a A Song. Thirty years later it's still my opinion that this was the greatest popular orchestra the world has ever known. The delicacy of the string scoring, the dynamic shading of the whole miniature symphony orchestra, the sheer power of the big band (when it played the big numbers from the civilian band's repertoire couldn't you just tell the difference?) were literally perfection in music. We in Britain were truly fortunate to have Major Miller and his American Band Of The AEF (as it was called here) broadcasting so often, playing troop concerts both in the field and at the Queensberry Services Club (now the London Casino), and I can even now recall the sense of sheer disbelief with which I heard the news on Christmas Day 1944 that Miller was reported missing. The band's tour of Europe, which he had been on his way to organise when his plane was lost, carried on till mid-1945 conducted by Sergeant Jerry Gray on broadcasts and Sergeant Ray McKinley on stage.

A rare photograph of a wartime broadcast by **Captain Robert Farnon and the Canadian Band Of The AEF,** with singer Joanne Dallas (at right). (*Robert Farnon*)

Miller's personal influence was still too real and too close for the band to suffer by his absence, and it was only in later years that Gray and McKinley, among many others, found that merely recreating the notes wasn't enough.

As well as the Miller band there were Captain Robert Farnon and the Canadian Band Of The AEF and Sergeant Major George Melachrino and the British Band Of The AEF, known as The Orchestra In Khaki. Here again both orchestras were completely un-commercial, assembled from the cream of each army's musicians, the leaders free to develop ideas and techniques which would serve them well in the postwar years. While George Melachrino, formerly vocalist/saxophonist with Carroll Gibbons at the Savoy, emphasised the more theatrical and neo-symphonic type of light music both in the army and in later years, Bob Farnon, a master of every type of music, has always been one of the few orchestral conductor-arrangers with a thorough knowledge of jazz and the ability to write relaxed, swinging lines for brass, saxes and rhythm even in his largest 'concert' orchestra and, what's more important, inspire the musicians to play them in a swinging manner. Having ten brass and six saxes to play with in his Canadian Army Band probably helped! Wartime Britain had another musical treat with a visit from Sam Donahue and his American Navy Band (formerly Artie Shaw's) which many critics regarded as a better swing band than Glenn Miller's, and this was the basis of a civilian outfit formed by Donahue on his discharge from the service. The Navy Band's pianist had been Claude Thornhill, who remained in the Pacific to carry on his activities with other navy groups, including one with actor Jackie Cooper on drums and Dennis Day as vocalist. Even the US Coast Guards had a thirty-piece orchestra led by Lieutenant Rudy Vallee, with his second in command Chief Petty Officer Jimmie Grier, former Gus Arnheim arranger and himself bandleader at the Cocoanut Grove after Arnheim's departure. Harpist in the Coast Guards band was Robert Maxwell, composer of 'Ebb Tide' and 'Shangri La', who has also been known to dub for Harpo Marx on movie soundtracks.

Back on the home front the band business was booming and there were always plenty of hotels, clubs and ballrooms to accommodate all the bands and the people who wanted to dance or listen to them. The early forties were notable for any number of excellent dance bands combining the elements of swing music and increasingly sophisticated arrangements of the good songs that were being written in ever-increasing numbers with the advent of songwriters such as Frank Loesser, Alec Wilder, Johnny Mercer, Jule Styne and Sammy Cahn, Hugh Martin and Ralph Blane, Jimmy Van Heusen and Johnny Burke, not to mention the continuing output of the leading writers of the thirties. Teddy Powell was more successful as a songwriter than a bandleader, but his band was better than most of his songs, of which 'Take Me Back To My Boots And Saddle' is a fairly representative example. Former Abe Lyman guitarist, Powell started out in 1939 in full-blooded swing style with scores by Bob Mersey, Ray Conniff and Henry Wells, but like many others he found this no-compromise approach hardly a viable proposition, and settled for leading a good dance band with just enough swing numbers in his programmes to keep the fans reasonably happy. It was this kind of compromise that ensured a long life for any band that could adapt itself to any location throughout the forty-eight States, and while few of the emergent leaders from the ranks achieved any permanent distinction their bands were generally musical in the extreme, entirely typical of the forties dance band scene, and possibly much more versatile than their occasional record releases would indicate.

At the time of writing there is a plethora of LP releases of forties broadcasts by the leading dance and swing bands consisting almost entirely of material never before recorded. Quite possibly the legality of these transcriptions, all issued by independent companies,

Charlie Spivak, one of the finest lead trumpets in the business, and leader of an equally fine band characterised by his beautiful open tone.

may be as dubious as the recording quality, but certainly the programme details of these albums give a fascinating insight into the range and scope of the most unlikely bands, and reveal just exactly how little the average dance band's commercial record output was representative of its true capabilities. Bobby Byrne took his trombone out of the Jimmy Dorsey band and built his own orchestra founded on Don Redman arrangements; Tony Pastor, a sidekick of Artie Shaw since their days in the sax section of Irving Aaronson's Commanders, left the Shaw organisation during one of the leader's retirements and never returned, keeping his own band going till the mid-fifties without making too much impact (other than by his use of Betty and Rosemary Clooney as singers in the late forties). Billy Butterfield, Randy Brooks and Sonny Dunham, known for their spectacularly melodic trumpet solos with Bob Crosby, Les Brown and the Casa Loma respectively, all tried to emulate Harry James's success without making it on the same scale, although Butterfield did well with a Gold Disc for 'Moonlight In Vermont' with its beautiful Margaret Whiting vocal. Charlie Spivak, whose open horn had similarly sparked the bands of Bob Crosby, Ray Noble and Jack Teagarden among others, was more successful. Heresy though it may be, there were times when his gorgeous tone and less effusive style were more acceptable than Harry James's, and the richness of the orchestral ensemble was particularly appealing. If, as I claimed a while back, Erskine Hawkins's was the archetypal coloured swing band, then Spivak's was the band which to me most surely represents the 'straight' dance music of the forties. Just to hear one of Spivak's recordings fixes the listener firmly and irrevocably in that one time and place. Bobby Sherwood was a trumpet-playing leader (also a guitar-trombone-piano playing and singing leader, but enough's enough!) who didn't try and follow in the James footsteps. He had a good big band that did all sorts of things from the roisterous 'Elks' Parade' to the progressive and moody 'Sherwood's Forest', and last cropped up in the film *Pal Joey* as a bandleader miming to Nelson Riddle's soundtrack music.

Glenn Miller's loyalty to old friends was legendary, and as he helped Charlie Spivak in his first solo venture, so he encouraged and helped finance Hal McIntyre, whose alto had led the Miller saxes since the band's inception and gave an identifying sound to McIntyre's own band which, again, did well without being too well-known outside the United States. Then there was Jerry Wald, a clarinettist whose band as well as himself played in the Artie Shaw style, although by the fifties he had a much more modern sounding outfit. Funny thing, although I saw the Wald band in person I can't remember a thing about it. It made absolutely no impression whatsoever whereas the Louis Prima band, seen the same week, still lingers in my mind. Positive badness is, I suppose, always more memorable than mere blandness and Prima did have a pretty bad band, but it was entertaining enough on its own level, portraying such gems of the songwriter's art as 'Please No Squeeza Da Banana', 'Josephine No Lean On Da Bell' and 'Angelina, The Waitress From The Pizzaria'. Originally a good New Orleans trumpeter, Prima brought musical and comic vulgarity to a fine art, and in so doing sold himself and his band to a public that maybe didn't like big bands too much. They also played boogie novelties and flagwavers and in a way the very roughness of the band was endearing. And, of course, Prima's gravel voice has endured,

Alvino Rey was using electronic guitar effects to sell his band thirty-five years ago, but personally preferred more uncommercial sounds. He seems to have had a gift for spotting arranging talent—Nelson Riddle, Frank de Vol, Jerry Fielding, Ray Conniff, Billy May, Neal Hefti and Johnny Mandel all worked for him in 1942! (*RCA Records, New York*)

through the Las Vegas years with his then wife Keely Smith and Sam Butera and the Witnesses, and now on Disney soundtracks. Alvino Rey was a showman of a different kind. Weaned in the Horace Heidt aggregation, he was no Latin type but a Scots-Irish-American whose real name was Al McBirney. When he left Heidt in 1938 he took with him the singing King Sisters and arranger Frank De Vol, adapted his electric guitar to include vocal effects, and set up in California as a show band. Later in the war he joined the swinging set with an even bigger band and scores by Billy May, Nelson Riddle, Neal Hefti, Ray Conniff and Jerry Fielding. The outstanding jazz trumpeters from the Ellington and Krupa bands, Cootie Williams and Roy Eldridge, also fronted their own bands in 1944-6, big, torrid swing bands built around the leaders' horns, and tenor sax Georgie Auld, who had had his first taste of leadership when he assumed control of the 1939 Artie Shaw orchestra, also bowed in with a powerful, uncompromising jazz band which at first changed its personnel as often as Auld changed reeds. In and out of the band for various engagements and recording dates went such distinguished guests as Dizzy Gillespie, Billy Butterfield, Errol Garner, Trummy Young, Chubby Jackson and Serge Chaloff, but it finally settled down in late 1945, and with the addition of Sarah Vaughan and arranger Tadd Dameron, Auld's mixed band (how those racial barriers had fallen since Goodman's pioneering efforts!) was highly regarded.

It is particularly frustrating that so many of these fine bands were active at a time when the recording industry was in a state of flux, and are not well represented on record. Many new bands appeared during 1942-4 when the recording ban imposed by the American Federation Of Musicians was in force, and still others were victims of the system whereby the big three record companies, RCA Victor, Columbia and Decca, had the business pretty well tied up. Capitol Records, founded by executive Glen Wallichs and song writers Buddy

Notable, if for nothing else, as the only left-handed violinist fronting a band, **Johnny Long** was a typical hotel band leader of the forties who worked successfully without becoming a legendary name.

De Sylva and Johnny Mercer, came along in 1942 with big ideas, but had to coast along on whatever stockpile of recordings they had until the end of the ban, when they emerged as a serious rival to the big three, with their roster of top artists including the King Cole Trio and the bands of Stan Kenton, Billy Butterfield, Freddie Slack, Paul Whiteman and Cootie Williams, to which they later added Billy May and Ray Anthony. This virtual monopoly of the business afforded an opportunity to a host of small companies which recorded bands prolifically but, limited by inadequate studio space, a lack of technical expertise, the shortage of raw materials, overcrowded pressing plants and restricted distribution, few of these wartime recordings which could have given us more insight into the big band scene have survived. In odd cases the copyrights have been purchased by larger companies, but have changed hands so many times in the past thirty years that trying to trace them would be a discographer's nightmare.

There was always a demand for the sort of conservative dance music that remained untouched by the changes of fashion. The kind provided by Johnny Long (the dance band world's only left-handed violinist?); Carmen Cavallaro who played excellent piano but never had more than a very good society band; Frankie Carle (another former Heidt Musical Knight) who wrote good songs like 'Sunrise Serenade' and 'Falling Leaves' and had a good competent band to play them; Johnny Messner, who finally gave up the perils of ownership for security as deputy leader for Vincent Lopez, who was as established in the forties as he had been in the twenties and thirties; and Eddie Howard, the ex-Dick Jurgens singer who had a big hit with 'To Each His Own' but remained better known as a singer than for his band, though he never achieved the eminence of Vaughn Monroe, the biggest voice of the forties. Not the best, just the biggest. Referred to variously as 'the man with muscles in his voice' and 'the voice with hairs on its chest', Monroe sang with the tone, warmth, passion, vibrancy and swing of a moribund Nelson Eddy. But the public liked him enough to buy a million copies of each of his records of 'Racing With The Moon', 'There I've Said It Again', 'Ballerina' and 'Riders In The Sky'. It may be perverse of me, but I didn't dislike Monroe. His voice matched his band's wall-to-wall blanket of sound and he was better than his comedy vocalist Ziggy Talent. Monroe survived the demise of the big bands because of his singing, finally going into Westerns as an actor.

Back in Britain the Squadronaires had set new standards, and dance music was given another shot in the arm by the regular broadcasting schedule allotted to Geraldo and his

Geraldo. (*EMI Records*)

Orchestra who, as far as my memory goes, must have been on the air every day of the week. Certainly no band before or since had such a marvellous showcase, and in this instance it was completely justified. A favourite since the twenties when Gerald Bright and his Orchestra were heard by Northern listeners from the Majestic Hotel, St Annes-on-Sea, Geraldo had progressed through the Gaucho Tango stage to the show selections of his 'Concert Orchestra' of the late thirties. Still he had no particular reputation as a modernist until those wartime programmes when he found himself with the cream of session musicians to pick from (just a few of the embryo bandleaders who played with Gerry were Ted Heath, Wally Stott, George Evans, Nat Temple, Leslie 'Jiver' Hutchinson, Eric Tann and Harry Hayes), a public eager to hear the newest and best of American swing, and the arrangers who could present the band in an individual way, particularly George Evans, whose use of woodwinds was unique. The Tip Top Tunes Orchestra, a big band with strings, was heavily influenced by the Miller army band, and some of Wally Stott's scores of traditional and standard tunes were skilfully conceived in Jerry Gray style (though I feel this was more the leader's idea than that of Stott, one of Britain's most brilliant arranger-composers). But whether being original or merely reflecting American trends, Geraldo brought musicianship, good taste and immaculate presentation to British dance music and set a standard by which all bands were henceforth to be judged. Smaller jazz and swing groups were heard on the

BBC's *Radio Rhythm Club*, the resident band being Harry Parry and his Radio Rhythm Club Sextet, whose allegiance to the Goodman Sextet couldn't have been more obvious. The BBC also adapted to its own needs NBC's *Chamber Music Society Of Lower Basin Street*, a somewhat pompous show allegedly devoted to jazz roots with leaders Henry Levine and Paul Laval and weekly guest stars of the calibre of Dinah Shore, Lena Horne and Sidney Bechet. The British version had a less self-conscious approach and some good swing music from Phil Green and his band. Green, a studio conductor who had recorded under many different names during the thirties and forties (he was Don Felipe for Latin music, Joe Paradise for Hawaiian, etc.), used top session men for this programme, and was also responsible for some purely functional but quite pleasant dance music when Decca Records created a *Music While You Work* series of records for factory use.

One of the same school of recording leaders was Harry Leader, a saxophonist and clarinettist in many early bands before joining Sid Phillips for an overseas tour. He originally formed a recording band for Crystalate before he began selling records in hundreds of thousands for the Broadcast and Eclipse labels. This was profitable for him as a session conductor, but as the records sold in Woolworth's for 6d (5 cents) each I don't imagine the question of royalties came into it. With EMI he had a better deal, although still not making a name for himself since he appeared on labels as Wally Bishop and his Band, Max Murray and his Orchestra, The International Novelty Orchestra and dozens of other pseudonyms. He first became a working bandleader when he took up residency at the Hammersmith Palais in 1940, later moving to the Astoria Ballroom where he shared the stand with Jack White and his Band. Harry Leader never had one of the top bands, never did anything spectacular, but he knew his business inside out. Mantovani was also very much a dance band leader in the forties, and though he never had any pretensions to leading a swing band he used good musicians for broadcasts and recordings and with the ever-reliable Alan Kane singing he made some pleasant dance-band-with-strings records. It seems incredible now, but for many years Mantovani and his Orchestra played at Butlin's holiday camps.

The sideman-turned-leader syndrome was not as evident here as in the USA but it did happen. Ronnie Munro, a highly competent arranger responsible *inter alia* for Ambrose's memorable 'When Day Is Done', took a band on the road, as did singer Leslie Douglas— he had a minor success in 1947 when his record of 'Open The Door Richard' was played night after night on the American Forces Network throughout Europe. Billy Thorburn, for many years pianist with the Savoy Orpheans under Debroy Somers and Carroll Gibbons (and, I believe, the first British pianist to play 'Rhapsody In Blue' in concert), had a unique little combo called The Organ The Dance Band And Me. An extrovert stylist, Bill's flashy piano didn't always blend with the staid cinema organ of H. Robinson Cleaver, and musically the combination was doomed from the start. But Billy Thorburn, one of the warmest human beings I ever knew, was liked by the public as well as by his colleagues, and kept a solo piano act going until music hall died under him. As one who, from 1940 to the mid-fifties, joined him in the artists' bar of theatres from Aberdeen to Chiswick, it was no surprise to me when his retirement was spent running a pub, until his death in the early seventies.

Eric Winstone was twenty when he led his first band at the Spanish Club in London in 1935 but, addicted to piano accordions, he not only did a solo stage act but composed for the instrument and wrote for journals devoted to it. Fortunately he was swing-minded and in 1940 formed a neat quartet, also fronting the London Accordion Band, which wasn't quite so hip. His 'Oasis', 'Stagecoach', 'Pony Express' etc. weren't jazz but good big band vehicles, the equivalent of the pieces Sid Phillips had written for Ambrose a decade pre-

Eric Winstone and his Orchestra at Butlin's Holiday Camp in the mid-40s. Alan Kane is at the microphone; Roy Marsh on drums. (*Alan Kane*)

viously. Then suddenly Eric Winstone and his Orchestra appeared, one of the first to use five brass and five saxes, playing a well-ordered and efficient brand of dance music that he supplied on records and in person (he was another long-term resident at Butlin's) until just before his death in 1974. Even this long service couldn't match that of Oscar Rabin who, with his partner Harry Davis, assembled his first quintet in 1924 at the Palace Hotel, Southend, under the aegis of Marius B. Winter. Augmenting to a nine piece, Rabin and Davis returned to London, finally settling in at the Royal Palace Hotel where they supported American visitors like Hal Kemp and Paul Specht and their orchestras. With Joe Loss they replaced Billy Cotton at the Astoria Ballroom, now being known as The Romany Dance Band, a name they retained until the forties when they settled on the name Oscar Rabin and his Band with Harry Davis, Oscar, a short, bald figure, playing bass sax while Davis, tall, elegant and a natural showman, fronted the band. It was well populated with singers, including Bob Dale, a handsome, masculine and stylish singer who should have become a big solo name but didn't, Diane, and Beryl Davis, Harry's daughter who later became a big name in the States. There was also a 'straight' Polish tenor, Jan Zalski, who sang entirely unsuitable numbers for a band show, but was introduced by Davis with a great deal of schmaltz as 'our brave Polish ally'. The 1946 Rabin band was the best of all, its saxes achieving a distinctive timbre through the luscious tone and vibrato of lead alto Ken Mackintosh. It specialised in cover versions of swing hits like 'Hamp's Boogie Woogie' and did them with as much conviction as almost any British band could muster. I say 'almost', because in 1944 Britain did get itself a real second-to-none swing band, one that even took America by storm.

Ted Heath had been a sturdy section trombonist with leading dance bands and on many record dates, although one of his earliest public appearances was as a busker in the streets of London during the depression, after a job with Will Marion Cook's Southern Syncopated Orchestra had folded. The coincidence that sounds like something out of a film script is that he was busking outside the Queen's Hall when he was heard by Jack Hylton, who just happened to have a trombone vacancy in his Queen's Hall Roof Orchestra. Bert Firman, Van Phillips, Sidney Lipton, Howard Jacobs, Jay Wilbur, and George Scott Wood all used the services of this adaptable musician, who was best known for his part in Ambrose's famous trombone trio with Lew Davis and Tony Thorpe. He was a fixture in Geraldo's wartime orchestra when the success of 'That Lovely Weekend' and 'I'm Gonna Love That Guy', two songs he and his wife had written, gave him the financial independence to put

Ted Heath And His Music. The sensational postwar band that put British swing music on the American map, shown here playing at the Palladium. (inset left to right) Its crowd-pulling triumvirate of talented singers, **Dickie Valentine, Lita Roza** and **Dennis Lotis.** (*Pye Records, British Lion Films*)

some of his ideas about big band music into practice. Initially he used an ad hoc band but, as the end of the war released musicians from the services, Ted Heath built a permanent organisation whose original personnel included Kenny Baker, Reg Owen, Johnny Gray, Ronnie Scott, Dave Shand, Harry Roche and Jack Parnell, all future leaders of their own orchestras. Determined to have a showcase for completely non-commercial music, Heath hired the London Palladium for a short series of a fortnightly show called *Sunday Night Swing Session* which, in the event, ran for years. By 1950 Ted Heath And His Music had reached an unassailable position and, with his all-star vocal team of Dickie Valentine, Dennis Lotis and Lita Roza appealing to the teenagers, he literally presented something for everyone. And he never lowered his standards. When the Musicians' Union ban on the interchange of British and American bands came to an end in 1955 Heath embarked on a series of American tours, in which his reputation stood as high as it did at home. A meticulous musical director, Ted Heath employed arrangers who wrote to his specifications, trained his musicians to the highest pitch of efficiency, yet remained himself the most self-effacing of bandleaders. No showmanship, no gift of the gab. He stood slightly hunched in front of this great swinging band, a stocky grey-haired man indicating directions with a flick of the finger rather than orthodox conducting. One had the feeling he would rather not be there but had to come along because the audience expected it. The shy man who told me so sorrowfully in 1944, 'Since I have had my own band other leaders won't play my songs', justified his actions and stifled all such petty jealousies by giving Britain the best band it had ever had.

The Heath band was most often compared with that of Les Brown, one of the few to make it through to the present day, latterly as musical director for Bob Hope, whose sponsorship has enabled Brown to keep a band together for nearly forty years. It started out as the Duke University Blue Devils in 1936, and when his sidemen returned to college Les, at twenty-five rather older than they, went on as arranger for Larry Clinton and Isham Jones, before taking over the Joe Haymes orchestra (Tommy Dorsey had taken over the first Haymes band a few years before, you may recall). By 1940 Brown had made it to that Mecca of big bands, the Glen Island Casino, with a sixteen year old singer named Doris Day, whose appearances with the band over the next few years coincided with her marriage problems. In 1945 Les and Doris had a big hit with 'Sentimental Journey', and when she left to do other things the band sold another million records of 'I've Got My Love To Keep Me Warm' in 1948-9—a tune they had actually recorded in 1943. That has got to be the 'sleeper' of all time! Les Brown and his Band of Renown reached their peak in 1953 at the Hollywood Palladium and the live performances recorded there, plus later studio albums for Capitol, are as good as anything produced by the Swing Era. I feel personally that Les Brown, together with Claude Thornhill, was responsible for possibly the finest swinging dance music of all time.

The reader is at liberty to disagree about Brown, but I don't think anyone who really knows music will quarrel with my assessment of Thornhill's place in the hierarchy. It's quite simple. He had a most musicianly, subtle, inventive, individual and completely beautiful orchestra. Delicacy, dynamics, tone colour, swing—Thornhill's was a truly progressive band, progressive in a sensitive, stylish manner rather than aggressively modern. With all these qualities, of course, it wasn't always a great public success. During the thirties Thornhill had gained professional renown for his work as a pianist on jazz sessions and with the Ray Noble and Glenn Miller band, for his skilful versions of traditional songs for Maxine Sullivan, and for his studio work with Andre Kostelanetz. (He and George Bassman founded the wonderfully evolved and involved Kostelanetz style of the mid-thirties before the conductor became more neo-classical in his settings of popular tunes.) When he went out on his own in 1939—another ex-Miller sideman who received practical encouragement from his old boss—Thornhill himself shared the arranging with Bill Borden and Gil Evans, but Evans (noted for his creation of the Miles Davis big band sound known as 'The Birth Of The Cool') himself insisted he wrote for Thornhill at the leader's instructions and that it was the Claude Thornhill band, as far back as 1941, which first played cool jazz, although no one knew it at the time. After Thornhill's navy service most of his old musicians returned to the fold, itself a tribute to his leadership and the warm personal regard felt for him as a man. There was also Fran Warren, whose emotional yet intensely musical style was echoed in later years by such singers as Toni Arden, Eydie Gorme and even, in a way, Barbra Streisand. The Thornhill-Warren 'Sunday Kind Of Love' is one of the all-time greats, and was one of the mere handful of 78s ever issued in Britain, where the neglect of Claude Thornhill on microgroove is nothing short of criminal. With jazz alto Lee Konitz and trumpeter Red Rodney the band did orchestral versions of bebop features like 'Anthropology' and 'Yardbird Suite', and in the fifties recorded a batch of Gerry Mulligan scores, all of which showed that, not only was it a great ballad orchestra, it was by no means negligible as a swing band. Claude Thornhill's later years were less happy musically, doing mood music albums and working with small pick-up bands round the country.

Not all the bands of the forties were as advanced and tasteful as Thornhill's, and there were signs that the Swing Era, in the second half of its colourful decade, was in danger of becoming stale. Too many bands copying others, too many—even topliners—featuring swing numbers that were little more than riffs or trite tunes with an arranger's veneer that barely concealed the banality; material which, although superficially attractive as jukebox fodder, was doing little to advance the cause of popular music. Musicians and fans alike were ready, even avid, for something new that would jolt dance and swing music out of the rut they felt it was in. The world was awaiting Stan Kenton and Woody Herman, Boyd Raeburn and Dizzy Gillespie, and when they arrived with their big band revolution they blazed a trail a mile wide; but one that very few followed and that ultimately led to the end of the line for big bands, though we didn't see it that way at the time. Whatever the final result, whether 'progressive jazz' did kill the band business or whether economic, social and other extra-musical factors would have killed it anyway, these bands made thrilling music. Yet, paradoxically, some of it has dated far more than the swing and jazz of an older era; but it did make an indelible mark on the history of the big bands. Virtuosity was the keynote, and although most of the modern jazz soloists of later years evolved from the progressive bands it was the ensemble displays and the writers' notes which were all-important.

Although Stan Kenton is regarded as the High Priest of progressive jazz he was far from being the founder of the movement. Surprising though it may seem, singer Billy Eckstine must be credited as an originator of the new styles in big band music, not only for his involvement with Earl Hines described in the previous chapter but for the inception of his own big bebop band when he left Hines in 1944. With Dizzy Gillespie as musical director he staffed the band with bop musicians like Charlie Parker, Dexter Gordon, Miles Davis, Howard McGhee and Art Blakey, took on Sarah Vaughan as his singing partner, and set out to storm the ramparts of big band orthodoxy. From what we have heard on the few atrociously recorded and badly pressed discs the Eckstine band made, it was a wild, exciting band that just happened to be too wild and exciting for consumption by any but musicians, and without good records and mass appreciation it couldn't last. The irony is that just two years later, with the public ear more attuned to way-out sounds, Dizzy Gillespie, with the same sort of band, made the jazz history that Billy Eckstine should

Stan Kenton and his mid-forties band that defied Swing Era convention and gave impetus to the short-lived vogue for 'progressive jazz'. Left to right: Trumpets: Johnny Anderson, Buddy Childers, Ray Wetzel, Ken Hanna, Chico Alvarez; trombones: Skip Layton, Harry Forbes, Kai Winding, Milt Bernhart, Bart Varsalona; saxes: Red Dorris, Boots Mussulli, Al Anthony, Bob Gioga, Bob Cooper; Eddie Safranski (bass); Shelley Manne (drums); Stanley Newcombe Kenton (Piano/leader).

have made. Stripped down to fundamentals, it was really an augmented development of the music Diz and Charlie Parker had made with their epochal small groups, and although reissues of the 1946 Gillespie band now sound almost conventional their impact at the time was quite shocking. Not always together, not always in tune, the band still had a freedom of movement, a fresh spirit that compensated for the technical imperfections in frantic pieces like 'Emanon' and 'Things To Come'. And always there was Diz himself, no technical faker like so many bop musicians, but a well-schooled trumpeter who had come up the hard way from Cab Calloway and Teddy Hill to Woody Herman and Boyd Raeburn, and who had the technique to convey to others his exploration of new worlds of musical expression.

Meanwhile Stan Kenton was still trying to achieve his own 'progressive' ideals, the ambitions he had always had far ahead of the sort of commercial dance music he had played and scored with the bands of Everett Hoagland and Gus Arnheim in the thirties. The orchestra that would eventually express his thoughts took shape in 1941 at the Rendezvous Ballroom, Balboa Beach—a dance band obviously, but one that jumped more than most. His own writing produced great thick chords for the ensemble, a pounding rhythm and a staccato style of phrasing that sounded either ponderous or new and exciting according to the listener's viewpoint. I still find those early Decca records of 'Taboo', 'Adios' etc. interesting, mainly because the sound was unlike any other and good or bad it was still Kenton's own. Even then he emphasised the quality of the saxophone section in 'Reed Rapture' and 'Opus In Pastels' (the later 'Etude For Saxophones' was in the same vein), the section given a personal sound by the vibrato of lead alto Jack Ordean. However ambivalent my attitude to Kenton I always return to these for sheer musical beauty. When he joined Capitol Records for his first 1943 recordings of 'Eager Beaver' and 'Artistry In Rhythm' something new had been added—Capitol's resonant recording quality which became an integral part of the Kenton 'sound'. These, with 'Southern Scandal' and 'Painted Rhythm' were good swingers with that extra Kenton touch that gave a new look to the basic Swing Era style. (Incidentally, Capitol had no British outlet until 1949, and those of us who squirrelled away imported pressings found ourselves in great demand among suddenly new-found friends.) Anita O'Day and June Christy had given the band glamour and the sort of powerful vocals that could compete with all that brass, and it was still, nominally at least, functioning as a dance band when Pete Rugolo joined the arranging staff of 1947 and the 'progressive' bit really began. In retrospect much of the 'progress'

Woody Herman and his Orchestra. For close on forty years, since the original 'Band That Plays The Blues', Woody has been creating new 'Herman Herds' with that flair for leadership that can turn young musicians into a superbly blended unit almost overnight. (*Jazz Monthly*)

seems merely pretentious (it was pretentious then, but who could argue with success?), as in the string-laden 'Innovations' orchestra, (though I did like 'Theme For Sunday') with which Kenton invaded the concert field. It came to a head with Bob Graettinger's 'City Of Glass', a whole album of abstractions that wouldn't have meant a thing if you studied it for a hundred years. Then suddenly in the mid-fifties, just as Stan Kenton made history by being the first American band to play commercially on British soil for twenty years, he returned to modern swing, with some help from Gerry Mulligan scores, and ever since has pursued a middle path between jazz and modernity.

If Kenton's neo-classicism was little more than Stravinsky-and-water, how much more so were some of the works George Handy created for Boyd Raeburn? A former society band leader who became addicted to jazz, Raeburn plunged into the big band scene with all the fervour of the convert, and with everything against him. His music was too advanced for the public, he chose the wrong time to maintain a big band in the wrong locations, his all-star policy led to personality clashes, but he ranks with Kenton and Herman in trying to chart a new course for big band music. His 1944 records for Grand were as a dance band, good but typical of many others of the period, but with the addition of Eddie Finckel as arranger he produced his best jazz work. It was George Handy, however, who gave the Boyd Raeburn band its legendary reputation. Originally Ellington-influenced, his music became more and more complex and dissonant, and his insistence on filling each three-minute score with the sum of his vast musical knowledge proved disturbing to dedicated as well as casual listeners, and his more horrendous scores now sound as pompous as a latter-day Whiteman. His replacement by Johnny Richards and Ralph Flanagan put the emphasis on melody embellished by woodwinds and harp, and the 1946 recordings for Ben Pollack's Jewel label are pretty without being merely bland. A couple of attempted comebacks in the fifties failed, and Raeburn died in 1966 after being in retirement for years. He didn't alter the course of big band jazz, and didn't always succeed in what he was trying to do, but his failures were more interesting than the successes of lesser men, and his neglect in the annals of big band music is unforgivable.

Which leaves us with the biggest name of all, in whose hands jazz leapt forward so successfully that it is still functioning when most of the others have gone. We met Woody Herman and his Band That Plays The Blues in the middle of the Swing Era and left them in the early forties as a satellite of the Shaws and Goodmans. There was a transition period during the AFM recording ban (not so long as it was for other bands, for Decca came to terms with the Federation and recommenced recording in November 1943, a year ahead of other companies) during which Herman enlarged and revamped his band, initially because of draft problems but subsequently to inject new, modernist blood into the ranks. In 1943–4 the new men like Neal Hefti, Ralph Burns, Pete Candoli, Dave Tough, Flip Phillips and Bill Harris were infiltrating, but it was when the First Herd's recordings under a new Columbia contract came out in early 1945 that, as Alec Wilder wrote me at the time, 'the impact, in terms of a brand new conception, has been as shattering as was the Benny Goodman band in 1935.' As with Kenton and Capitol, so Columbia's resonant studios gave strength and depth to the fantastically accurate playing, the exciting scores of Hefti, Burns and Shorty Rogers, and, in fact, this whole new concept of big band music that made everything that had gone before seem dead as the dodo. Only those who were around at the time and bought these records when they were new, can appreciate my difficulty in trying to describe the overall impression this new band made. The staggering brilliance of five trumpets playing wild bop phrases in perfect unison in 'Caldonia', the powerful ensemble in 'The Good Earth' and 'Northwest Passage', Herman's sensuous alto and excellent vocals on ballads, always richly melodic but far from bland, the amazing virtuosity of 'Apple Honey'—but why go on? The fact that this wasn't merely a jazz band but a first-class orchestra by any standards was proved when Igor Stravinsky wrote his 'Ebony Concerto' for the Herman band and conducted its record debut. Succeeding Herds all contributed something, like the Second Herd with its much-copied Four Brothers sax section voicings created by Jimmy Guiffre and Al Cohn for the talents of Herb Steward, Stan Getz, Zoot Sims and Serge Chaloff. What number the current (1976) Herd is I have no idea, but Woody Herman is still out front, a man sixty-odd years young, leading, training and inspiring by his own example a new band of youngsters every other year; rather more pop-influenced now perhaps, but appealing to younger fans as well as those who remember those swinging years of the mid-forties when the First Herd proved the most cataclysmic discovery of the era.

The war years had given big bands their biggest ever audience, a public captured by the need for relaxation, entranced by the star vocalists who shared the limelight, and finally mesmerised by the sheer volume and technical brilliance of the Kentons, Hermans and Gillespies. How ironic that these factors which built up the band business during the war years should be those which would, in peacetime, militate against the bands and prove their downfall.

5 THE BEGINNING OF THE END THE POST WAR YEARS

There was no one specific reason for the postwar decline of the band business in America, although the last paragraph of the previous chapter gives an indication of the way things were going. Leaders who, aware of the vital need for wartime entertainment, had made financial demands that would have been considered exorbitant in earlier days, now found managements reluctant to meet their prices in view of declining audiences. Musicians, at a premium during wartime and able to command top salaries, also suffered from this financial cutback, especially when the return of their colleagues from the forces and war work created a situation whereby supply exceeded demand. In turn, reduced salaries created a reluctance to go out on the road, particularly when the really top line big band sidemen, experienced readers and adaptable to any style, could make more money as session men in radio, recording and film studios. These resident jobs enabled them to enjoy a degree of family life denied to them in the era of one-night stands; as far as the public was concerned, too, domesticity was replacing entertainment. The teenagers who had jitterbugged in the aisles at the Paramount, the couples who had romanced to Glenn Miller and Tommy Dorsey, the servicemen who had maybe had their first taste of swing with the Donahue, Shaw and Miller service bands, the fans who had bopped to Herman and Gillespie—their formative years were over, they were all just a little older, and freed from the perils and excitement of wartime were ready to settle down back home in a new life, or return to the old one, with marriage, children, mortgages, finance company repayments, all the responsibilities that would make a night out a special event rather than the norm.

Then there were musical reasons for the slow death of the big bands. When the 'progressive' outfits left dazed couples standing in mid-floor the dancers' thoughts inevitably returned to the nights when they had felt emotionally secure dancing and listening to the love lyrics sung so expressively by the good-looking boys and the girls who had first felt the glow of the spotlight as vocalists with the popular dance bands. They remembered Frank Sinatra and Jo Stafford, Bob Eberle and Helen O'Connell, Dick Haymes and Helen Forrest, Billy Eckstine and Sarah Vaughan, Perry Como and Marilyn Maxwell, Ray Eberle and Marion Hutton. They remembered Doris Day, Peggy Lee, Mel Tormé, Martha Tilton, Don Cornell, Ginny Simms and Margaret Whiting as their favourite band singers. They remembered the Pied Pipers, the Merry Macs, the King Sisters, the Modernaires, and the Clark Sisters when they were Tommy Dorsey's Sentimentalists. The singers weren't just one-chorus-and-out vocalists any more. They had paid their dues in the bands and gone on to MGM and 20th Century Fox, they starred at the Paramount and the Copacabana and now had their names above the orchestra on record labels. The big bands had discovered and groomed the singers, taught them to sing in tune and in tempo, given them a musical education and discipline they would never forget, and graduated them *summa cum laude*. They had also given them a public, one that was now about to forget the teachers and the schoolroom and elevate the pupils to stardom. The singers in their turn would be overtaken by the rock groups, but in the immediate postwar years it was their market.

I must not give the impression that there was a sudden decline in the popularity of bands. The writing may have been on the wall but their day was not yet over. Rather was there a change in musical appreciation, and although bands would continue to make million-selling records for the next decade there was a conspicuous absence of the big swing names. James, Miller, Dorsey and Shaw were replaced by Kay Kyser's 'Woody Woodpecker', Art Mooney's 'Four Leafed Clover', Russ Morgan and Blue Barron vying with 'Cruising Down The River', The Firko String Band's 'Heartbreaker', Freddie Martin's 'I've Got A Lovely Bunch of Coconuts', sundry Guy Lombardos and Vaughn Monroes, and a one-off hit with 'Near You' by an obscure bandleader from Nashville named Francis Craig. Quite definitely, things weren't what they used to be! Yet it was also a time for new bands, especially in Britain where a new Swing Era began as the American one ended. British fans, having received their baptism of swing music at first hand during the war with the invasion of American musicians, were a custom-built public for leaders who, inspired by Ted Heath's example, presented ever larger orchestras in which eight brass, five saxes and four rhythm became the average line-up. Many sidemen proved to be talented arrangers and in the Heath band alone the library was written within the band by trumpeter Kenny Baker, trombonist Lad Busby, saxist Reg Owen and pianist Norman Stenfalt, in addition to contributions from men like George Shearing and Robert Farnon who were happy to write imaginative scores for this fine orchestra.

The closing months of the war had seen the emergence of an impressive big band directed by Teddy Foster. Foster was playing trombone with Percival Mackey at fifteen, completing his musical education in Holland with Van 't Hoff's Virginians before building a reputation as a leading trumpet soloist with Syd Seymour, Billy Cotton, Ambrose and Jack Payne. He had made several attempts at bandleading, prewar with his Kings Of Swing, in 1939 at the Streatham Locarno and in 1943 at the Birmingham Casino, but the big band he formed in 1945 for the Royal Opera House, Covent Garden (in temporary use as a ballroom), was undoubtedly his most successful both musically and commercially, although he no longer featured himself on trumpet. Two 'hot' bands moving from the war years into peacetime were fronted by musicians from the band Ken Johnson had led at the Café De Paris. Clarinettist Carl Barriteau from Trinidad and trumpeter Leslie 'Jiver' Hutchinson from Jamaica may not have been completely uncompromising in their attitude to swing but this was understandable, for however knowledgeable and sophisticated swing fans were becoming they were still, as always, in the minority. But the leaders, who had both worked with Ambrose, Lew Stone and Geraldo since Johnson's death, were first-class soloists— Barriteau in particular was one of Britain's leading jazzmen and a regular poll winner—and men of taste in their selection of musicians and repertoire. Barriteau fronted a white band and Hutchinson a West Indian group, both of which played in a style that somehow managed to please the dancing public as well as the fans.

My own personal favourite was the George Evans Orchestra, the most individual, musicianly and colourful band ever heard in Britain. George Evans, who gained his first experience on tenor sax with Freddie Bretherton's band, is mentioned in Chapters 2 and 3 for his work in jazz and dance music. Serving with the Welsh Guards during the war, he wrote for and played with the Guards Dance Band, and in between spare-time sessions with Geraldo's orchestra he formed his first all-saxophone band, the Saxes and Sevens, for the Embassy Club, and led a large session band in four memorable Decca sides in preparation for the day when he made his debut as a civilian leader. With five trumpets, ten saxophones and four rhythm the orchestra was capable of an enormous range of tone colours, and the texture of the ensemble on ballads was a rewarding experience for anyone who appreciated true sonority and depth in a dance orchestra. As George Evans said later, 'I was working round the clock, making money hand over fist but with no time to enjoy it. Something had to give!' And his health did, with a long spell in a TB sanatorium during which the orchestra was led on tour by his brother Leslie. George had to give up playing jazz tenor sax, but in 1949 he formed a student orchestra and an experimental swing choir in which I took part. This latter never got beyond the experimental stage but so successful was his training of young musicians that the George Evans Orchestra once more became a reality, this time with a trombone section added. After a spell of one-nighters the band settled for a residency at the Oxford Galleries, Newcastle, in the early fifties, where it remained, giving local dancers the best dance music in the country, until George's eventual retirement.

Guitarist Vic Lewis, co-founder of the RAF Lewis-Parnell Jazzmen, was early on the postwar scene with a big band all too obviously founded on Lewis's undisguised admiration for Stan Kenton, whose British counterpart as master of progressive jazz he was determined to be. Although certain deficiencies tended to show up on records and broadcasts, it was an exciting band to hear in person, and Vic Lewis, a charming and well-liked man, was a good ambassador for British jazz. The Lewis band was, in retrospect, most notable as a nursery for such future bandleading talent as Ken Thorne, Johnny Keating, Gordon Langhorn (he became Don Lang in the Rock Era), Stan Reynolds, Arthur Greenslade, Ronnie Scott and Tubby Hayes. Long forgotten, but one band I always enjoyed seeing in person, was that of Tommy Sampson, a studious-looking Scot who fronted a progressive band that made even Vic Lewis sound tame. I don't honestly remember whether it ever recorded, and perhaps time has lent enchantment to my memories, but I do know that around 1948-9 an evening spent listening to the Tommy Sampson Orchestra was never wasted. Before he took over the Skyrockets from Paul Fenhoulet, trombonist Woolf Phillips (brother of Sid Phillips) had a musicianly, solidly swinging band, not as madly progressive as Lewis and Sampson but modern in the best sense. He later used some of his best scores with the Skyrockets (I still have a 78 of his 'Blue Skies', an arrangement that is everything good swing should be), but residency at the London Palladium gave him little opportunity other than occasional Sunday concert dates to prove his worth as one of the country's most underrated leader-arrangers.

Does anyone, I wonder, remember The Stardusters? Just five saxes and rhythm led by George Birch, they were a masterly little band with a lovely section sound and imaginative voicings that overcame the lack of a brass section. Cyril Stapleton, as described elsewhere, had the same line-up plus one trumpet and an affinity for the gospel according to Glenn Miller, which took over at Fischer's Restaurant from Frank Weir. One of the longest serving active musicians in Britain, Weir started as an army bandsman in 1925, entering the dance band world in 1934 with Jack Hylton, moving on to Howard Jacobs at the Savoy and following up as a sideman with Fred Hartley's Quintet, Sidney Lipton, Geraldo, Ambrose and Arthur Young. His first experience as a leader was in charge of HMV's recorded jam sessions in 1941 and he opened at the Bagatelle Restaurant the same year. He served as a ferry pilot with Air Transport Auxiliary and when discharged on medical grounds formed his Astor Club Seven. Opening at Fischer's he later took a big band on the road with George Shearing on piano and featuring his own clarinet lead, but managed to avoid any comparisons with Shaw or Goodman. Frank Weir made some good records for Decca with a large string section added to his normal complement, producing a pleasant if rather bland sound based loosely on the concept of dance music with strings inspired by Glenn Miller and carried on in peacetime by the civilian version of the AEF Orchestra. When Miller's army musicians stayed together after the war, presented by the Miller Estate and fronted by Tex Beneke, who had been such a vital part of the prewar band as tenor soloist and singer, no one could have foreseen that imitations of the Miller sound would be big business for nearly three decades to come. Or that this once valuable musical currency would be devalued by so many opportunists.

Obviously the state of the market was not such that Beneke and manager Don Haynes could maintain a working band on the same scale as the A E F Orchestra, and what emerged was a considerably slimmed-down version using the same arrangements, which it did very well. And though the recordings Beneke made for RCA lacked the sheer dynamic power of the original, we were pleased to make do with them until RCA unlocked the vaults ten years later and produced a five-record boxed set of 1943-4 recordings from the 'I Sustain The Wings' broadcasts, rehearsals and other sources. After a few years Beneke and the Miller Estate fell out over musical policy, and Tex forgot 'the sound' in his new, but less successful swing band. Don Haynes and Mrs Helen Miller might well have been happy to leave Glenn's music to history but for the rash of Miller-inspired bands that sprang up in the late forties and early fifties. This was nothing new. Even while the original Miller band was still operating, Bob Chester, whose records were issued alongside Miller's on RCA's Bluebird label, was copying the saxophone section sound, though he later dropped this in favour of a more original approach. But so long after Miller's death? There was some excuse for Jerry Gray who had after all been one of the creative forces behind the original band's rise to fame. So much Glenn Miller material was his anyway that he did a quite logical thing in forming a band to play his old scores the way he knew they should be played. Although singer Ray Eberle was never a very successful bandleader his own long association with Miller could, in a way, be considered an excuse for him to play and record tributes to his old boss. Even Ray Anthony, who had one of the best postwar bands, had spent a short time in the Miller trumpet section, though whether this tenuous connection warranted his copying the style is open to conjecture. But certainly Ralph Flanagan, an otherwise talented arranger for Tony Pastor, Boyd Raeburn, Hal McIntyre and Gene Krupa, had never had the remotest link with Miller. Yet of all the copyists his was the most blatant and successful plagiarism which earned big rewards for RCA and himself in the early fifties. Thus, with all this imitation music going on and others cashing in on a dead man's music, the Miller Estate was completely justified in reforming an official 'Glenn Miller Orchestra' twelve years after his death and sending it out under the direction of Ray McKinley, Glenn's long-term friend and associate in the Dorsey Brothers Orchestra and the Army Band. McKinley no longer played drums except in a feature spot, and proved an ideal front man with a fine sense of humour and great showmanship. Strictly speaking, this band of youngsters was no more authentic than any other, but with the use of Glenn's name and Mrs Miller's blessing it sold a kind of nostalgia that ensured standing room only when it did a tour of Britain around 1957. Audiences loved it as I did, and one felt for a while that with this sort of response there must be a market for professionally presented stage shows of dance bands playing good standard music. But it was an isolated instance, and as was proved when ex-Tommy Dorsey clarinettist Buddy De Franco took over the band in the mid sixties, it was the magic Miller name that was a draw rather than dance music *per se*.

In recent years De Franco has taken the band along some odd paths that I'm sure neither Miller nor his widow, were she still alive, would have approved. Now it's just another band owing a little to Glenn Miller, but not actually as good in performance as the British band of Syd Lawrence, which in 1975 is still filiing theatres and ballrooms and selling thousands of records with Miller imitations, to which Lawrence has recently added the sounds of other Swing Era bands. My own feelings about this are rather ambivalent. As I said earlier I don't want to hear imitations when records of the originals are still available. On the other hand it is a good sign that there should still be an audience for big band music, even at second-hand, and it does mean regular employment for musicians playing their own kind of music.

The 'ghost band' syndrome also extended to the Dorseys who, along with Miller, were

The success of the Glenn Miller 'sound' produced a rash of imitations after Miller's death, some officially sponsored by the Miller Estate but others more opportunist. **Bob Chester and his Orchestra** (*bottom left*) presented by Miller rival Tommy Dorsey, were doing a carbon copy as far back as 1940, while recording for the same Bluebird label as Miller. The first official Glenn Miller Orchestra (1946) was led by **Tex Beneke** (*above right*) (twenty-two year old Henry Mancini can be seen looking over the piano), and in later years by **Ray McKinley** (1956) (*top right*) and **Buddy de Franco** (1966) (*top left*). **Ralph Flanagan** (*left-second from top*) produced a commercially successful pastiche of the Miller sound in the early fifties, and at the time of writing **Syd Lawrence and his Orchestra** (*left-third from top*) are selling a carbon copy of the old Miller scores to British audiences. (*RCA Records, New York; EMI Records; Phonogram Records*)

the favourite commercial bands of the forties. The final Dorsey Brothers Orchestra was carried on after Tommy's death by the rapidly failing Jimmy and earned a Gold Disc for 'So Rare' under his name, but so ill was Jimmy Dorsey by this time that some of the alto solos on the parent album were actually played by Dick Stabile. Lee Castle (Lee Castaldo of the Tommy Dorsey band of the forties) left the trumpet section and took over after Jimmy's death while Warren Covington, former trombonist with Les Brown and Horace Heidt, led the 'Tommy Dorsey Orchestra' and turned out a big hit in 1958 with 'Tea For Two Cha Cha'. This had no connection with the Tommy Dorsey style but proved a further, if temporary, stimulus for the band business. In 1964 Sam Donahue came to Britain with a new version of the orchestra featuring Charlie Shavers and teaming the experienced Helen Forrest with the immature Frank Sinatra jnr, who didn't exactly recall his father's illustrious stint with the original band. Since Donahue's death the apparently perennial Tommy Dorsey Orchestra has visited us, again with Covington in charge.

For some reason the names of Ray Anthony and Billy May are usually linked in our memories of the fifties. They had played side-by-side in Glenn Miller's brass section and after the war both became contracted to Capitol Records. Their records were generally being issued coincidentally, but the bands had little in common except good musicianship. Anthony relied on Miller-ish ballad settings, his own trumpet solos adding a dimension the other copyists lacked. But it was also a good swing band and gained acceptance on its own merits until such time as the final recession in the business compelled Anthony to play club dates with a sextet. Billy May originally joined Capitol as an all-purpose musical director, his Swing Era experience as trumpeter, composer and arranger having been broadened by studio work on the radio shows of Red Skelton, Bob Crosby and Ozzie Nelson. He did everything from children's records to pop vocal accompaniments, and was eventually allowed to record with a hand-picked big band that gained attention through his gimmick of 'slurping saxes' in which exaggerated *portamenti* by the sax section gave the band a unique sound. This was his entrée to public acclaim and when it had served its purpose May went on to make a series of albums notable for the vital, jazz-influenced swing which had characterised his work in the forties, allied to a mordant wit which revealed itself in nearly everything he did. May tried his band out on the road but conditions were now such that it took little persuasion for him to hand over to Sam Donahue while he returned to the security of the studios. He wrote for films and TV and, after a heart attack, eased off still more into lecturing on music in colleges across the country. Had Billy May been able to organise a regular band at the peak of the Swing Era it would have been one of the all-time greats. For my money it was anyway, ad hoc band or not, and it is something of a paradox that two of the finest bands of all should have emerged after the big band scene had been written off.

The other fine band was the 1952-8 Sauter-Finegan Orchestra, which for sheer ensemble dynamism, tonal richness, and imagination has never been equalled before or since—except maybe by Claude Thornhill. The Sauter-Finegan Orchestra took it just that bit further than Thornhill, though, adding humour with the use of fifes, tuba, harp, oboes, kazoos, glockenspiel etc in quite outrageous effects that nevertheless sounded just right in context. Purists have complained that Sauter-Finegan wasn't a jazz band, but this would be like a classical writer nagging Sinatra for not singing opera. What Eddie Sauter and Bill Finegan did was to combine two of the greatest arranging talents of the Swing Era with some of New York's finest musicians and construct an *orchestra* to play advanced, witty, imaginative big band *music*. There were jazz solos and the nineteen-piece band swung mightily on rhythm numbers, but primarily it was a modern musical entertainment—not necessarily the direction in which they thought big band music as a whole should move but the way

Co-leaders of the legendary Sauter-Finegan orchestra of 1952–8, **Eddie Sauter** and **Bill Finegan** were two of the most musicianly and tasteful arrangers in the history of big band music. (*RCA Records*)

Johnny Dankworth and his Orchestra. (*Kenneth Pitt*)

they wanted their music to go. Bill Finegan had been an arranging mainstay of the Glenn Miller and Tommy Dorsey bands, while Eddie Sauter had gained a reputation as a writer far ahead of his time for his sensitive prewar work with Red Norvo, his thoughtful scores that gave Benny Goodman a new direction in 1940, and the ultra-modern style he created for Ray McKinley's sensational postwar band. Together these kindred spirits made beautiful music, and I mean that literally. The 'Doodletown' nonsense was good fun and some of their progressive jazz works could have shown Kenton the way, but I know of no musical moment comparable to the release of 'April In Paris' when Florence Fogelson's soprano tops the ensemble in a spine-chilling climax.

The early fifties saw Britain's postwar Swing Era recede as quickly as it had arrived, apart from the permanently inspiring example of Ted Heath; but new bands did still emerge to try and combat the changing tastes in popular music. Johnny Dankworth went out on a limb with an uncommercial big band that has managed to survive, at least as a recording unit, subsidised by the leader's film and concert writing. Although of orthodox instrumentation the band achieved a distinctive sound by incorporating the voicings of the Dankworth Seven in the ensemble in place of a conventional saxophone section. An un-compromising idealist, Dankworth is one of the few leaders to subsist on the loyalty of jazz fans, though it cannot be denied that the vocal presence of his wife Cleo Laine has been a big selling point. Drummer Jack Parnell left Ted Heath to form a band that did some nice work until he too succumbed to the lure of financial security as conductor at the London Palladium and eventually commercial TV's leading musical director. One of the brightest spots of the early fifties was provided by a sympathetic BBC producer, the late Pat Dixon, who originated a radio series which gave Kenny Baker and his Baker's Dozen complete freedom to do their own thing. Baker, the finest lead trumpet and soloist in British jazz, responded magnificently, and his Dozen produced a happy blend of swing and jazz owing allegiance to no particular style but rather utilising all he and his all-star cohorts had ever learned about jazz (a few years later it would have been known as 'mainstream'). Dixon also put Nat Temple and his Band in the subtle and genuinely funny comedy series *Breakfast With Braden* and *Bedtime With Braden*, though it's possible that Bernard Braden himself, a man with a wide knowledge of jazz and popular music, may have had a hand in the choice. Done without a studio audience, the shows drew a hilarious response from the Temple musicians and when singer-actor Benny Lee took me along to one of the recordings I found that the most hysterical laugh in the studio belonged to drummer Eric Delaney. I should have known. I had first worked with Eric in an RAF band at Madley in 1944. Just

Eric Delaney and his Orchestra. A latecomer to the big band field, but Eric's twin bass drums and tuned tympani provided the sort of showmanship (and a hit record of 'Oranges And Lemons') that kept him in business after others had fallen by the wayside. (*Kenneth Pitt*)

nineteen, he had already seen service with the Ambrose Octet, and over supper in the mess after the station dances we would talk unendingly about music. Listening to Geraldo on the radio one night Eric said, 'Marvellous band. I'm going to play with Gerry one day.' Four years later we met again—on a Geraldo broadcast. The year 1954 was hardly a good time for a new band to break into a moribund scene, but Eric Delaney forsook the security of the Geraldo organisation and did just that. It wasn't an enormous band, and decreased over the years, but realising the limitations of a conventional big band with Krupa-type showmanship, Eric centred the band round himself playing tuned tympani. Originality paid off when his first record, 'Oranges and Lemons', took off and provided a first-time hit for the only British band on the American-owned Mercury label.

In America it was more of an arranger's scene as men who had spent their lives writing for others saw the ever-expanding record industry and the introduction of the LP record as a medium for their own conceptions of modern swing music. Hence many big recording names of the past two decades have been bandleaders in name only, their sole function being to conduct all-star bands, selecting their personnel from the cream of Swing Era musicians resident in the studios (thus has the wheel turned full circle, back to the days of Ray Noble). The fact that the same circle of session men played on most of the records (there was one clique in New York and another in Hollywood) ensured good team work with a minimum of rehearsal time but, and here again this may be a purely personal reaction, the academic perfection of it all tended to detract from the effect of listening to a real live band. One knew it didn't exist outside the studio and may even have longed for an occasional mistake just to prove there were really people in there. In Los Angeles men like Shorty Rogers, Shelley Manne, Marty Paich and Dave Pell were responsible for 'West Coast Jazz', a somewhat enervated 'cool' variant depending largely on ensemble writing which occasionally swelled to big band proportions. Others like Jerry Fielding (as Jerry Feldman he had been Alvino Rey's arranger), Larry Sonn, Johnny Richards, Pat Williams and Terry Gibbs did occasional albums, while Henry Jerome spent some years producing a series of Decca records by his all-brass Commanders. Harry Zimmerman did a couple of interesting records with a huge band playing popular evergreens in march time, and Dixieland standards; Jackie Gleason put out under his name two excellent 'Velvet Brass' albums, really good big band music, as well as the Sy Oliver-scored 'Romantic Jazz' mentioned in Chapter Three. Former society maestro Enoch Light created Command Records and his own Project 3 label, both devoted to the ultimate in stereophonic (and later quadraphonic) sound, coming down heavily in favour of large bands built around a nucleus of New York sessioneers like guitarist Tony Mottola, pianist Dick Hyman and trombonist Urbie Green, who all did their own sessions plus working *in toto* in a revived version of Enoch's Light Brigade doing recreations of Swing Era hits. Light also brought back to the scene latterday bands of Sammy Kaye and Dick Jurgens. Though many Light productions erred on the side of technical gimmickry his contributions to our music were greater in the sixties and seventies than they ever were in his own heyday as a bandleader. Pete Rugolo did some interesting sessions for Mercury with all-trumpet, all-trombone and all-saxes bands, more commercial in content than his 'progressive' work with Kenton but models of ingenuity and taste. But not all the bands had vanished into the limbo of the recording studios, and in 1962 a special big band issue of *Downbeat* listed seventy-five top bands still on the road, a blend of veterans like Ziggy Elman, Nat Pierce, Louis Bellson, Ralph Marterie, Les and Larry Elgart (together and separately) and Buddy Morrow (who as Moe Zudekoff had been a sturdy trombonist with Bob Crosby, Artie Shaw and Tommy Dorsey); and newcomers like Claude Gordon, Herb Pomeroy and Sal Salvador few of whom have been heard from since.

Buddy Morrow. As Moe Zudecoff he played trombone with Sharkey Bonano, Bob Crosby, Tommy Dorsey and Artie Shaw. The more euphonious name suited his position as a leader who made some good records in the fifties before returning to studio work. (*EMI Records*)

In 1951 Neal Hefti drew on his experience as a founder member of the Herman Herd to present a band of his own with his wife Frances Wayne as singer. Despite his comparative failure it made a couple of good Coral albums and served as a prototype for the new style Hefti created for the Count Basie Orchestra, one that raised the struggling Basie to the hierarchy of postwar swing bands. Hefti wasn't alone, however, Ernie Wilkins also contributing notably to the Basie library in the mid-fifties followed by Quincy Jones, Benny Carter and others producing a sound that, no matter who the originator, was still unmistakably Basie's. Frequent changes of personnel have kept the band fresh and alive, and though not as strong on solo work as the thirties edition it made its name with wonderfully dynamic ensemble playing contrasting with the Count's own inimitable piano and what is still the most inspiring rhythm section in jazz. Elliot Lawrence was just out of university when he assembled his first band in Philadelphia, a mellow outfit of the Thornhill school which landed a spot at the Hotel Pennsylvania, New York in 1946. With scores by Gerry Mulligan, Tiny Kahn and Johnny Mandel, Lawrence's became one of the best modern bands, but in the perilous fifties he joined the ever-growing list of conductors who settled for a more tranquil life on Broadway and in the studios. In the early sixties it looked as if Peter Duchin might fill the gap left by the death of his father Eddy Duchin with a number of LPs featuring his piano and orchestra, but while his playing was more modern than Eddy's both it and the band lacked any positive virtues or vices. Quincy Jones wasn't a working bandleader for long, but the eighteen piece he formed in 1959 for a tour of Harold Arlen's *Free And Easy* was an all-star group by any standards and the means by which the ex-Hampton trumpet-arranger built a successful career as a recording supervisor and Hollywood writer.

Si Zentner had been more of a 'musicians' musician' than an object of fan worship when he played trombone with Les Brown and in studio orchestras, and he appeared to tempt

Elliot Lawrence. A thoroughly schooled musician, Lawrence had one of the most underrated bands of the late forties and fifties before taking his talents to Broadway as a theatre conductor.

fate by waiting until the sixties to front his own band. But he was lucky in that his recording of 'Lazy River', with a suggestion of a Twist beat, appealed to youngsters as well as swing fans, and since then he has gone on to prove that a swing band can still be big business. By including in his billing the slogan 'The band you see on the road is the band you hear on the record', Zentner tilted at the system whereby studio leaders would sometimes take inferior bands on tour. But in all the numerous attempts to 'bring the bands back', the one Swing Era musician to preserve the elements of big band music while meeting modern pop on its own terms is Ray Conniff. His name has appeared in various chapters of this book as trombonist and arranger for some of the biggest bands of the thirties and forties yet he never led a band of his own till he was forty. After war service he joined Columbia Records to write and conduct vocal arrangements, and in 1956 he gave the world a completely new concept of big band music by using a choir phrasing instrumentally, doubling up with the brass and sax sections. Coinciding with the advent of stereo, the recording quality lavished on the Conniff sound gave it a clarity and sharpness of definition that one wishes could have been accorded to the bands of the Swing Era who all too often suffered from inferior studio techniques and gritty shellac pressings. It was the music of the moment that record buyers wanted to hear even at the height of the Rock Era, yet, shorn of the trimmings, it was basically typical forties swing that somehow appealed to a brand new public. In recent years Conniff has tended to veer somewhat from paths of righteousness, descending to what have been little more than king-size pop group cover versions of current hits, with any orchestral accompaniment being purely nominal. But when the Ray Conniff Orchestra and Singers make personal appearances the leader does remember his roots; the big band is there with featured spots for such alumni of the forties as John Best on trumpet, Skeets Herfurt on sax, Johnny Guarnieri on piano and Conniff himself on trombone, reminding us that here is a man, an essential part of the contemporary scene, a million-record seller, who has been part of it all for nearly forty years. A link with the past—or a sign that some things never die?

✐ IT TAKES ALL KINDS

Preceding chapters have introduced the outstanding bands which for reasons of musician-ship, originality, popularity, or the qualities possessed by individual bandleaders, made the big band sound one of the dominant features of twentieth-century musical life. They formed the mainstream, so to speak.

But there are other tributaries to be explored, explicit categories of musical entertain-ment (and let us never forget for one minute that entertainment is what it's all about), some involving large orchestras of standard instrumentation playing music in a more specialised form, others involving smaller and less standardised groups. None of these bands was less important in the general scheme of things, or less successful in its own way, than the Dorseys and Ellingtons and Heaths. On the contrary, by doing their own thing and con-centrating on their appeal to one particular section of the market, many of these leaders proved highly durable. The *big* big bands hit the highspots and are assured of their role in posterity; but the Golden Age Of Dance Bands and the Swing Era lasted something like a decade and a half between them. Before, during and since those halcyon days there was also a mass market to be entertained, a public to whom 'Harlem Air Shaft' and 'Artistry In Rhythm' meant nothing, but who would faithfully support the *Billy Cotton Band Show* to the end. Every band mentioned in this chapter has its place in the story.

The Great Show Bands

We've seen how Paul Whiteman and Jack Hylton became the pioneers of stage band presentation, and their reputations as *the* great showmen of the dance band world have never been equalled. Perhaps not surprisingly in view of its long music hall tradition, Britain went in more for stage band shows than America, whose bands it is true made a healthy living in the thirties and forties on the stages of cinemas and theatres throughout the States. They did, however, concentrate more on the musical aspect, while British bands really put on a show with comedy, visual effects, dancing and singing—self-contained musical revues, in fact. The Jack Hylton band included singers Ella Logan and Pat O'Malley who went on to fame in America, and blind pianist Alec Templeton who also headed Stateside on the strength of his 'Bach Goes To Town' which Benny Goodman made a standard, while the comedy was handled by saxophonist Freddie Schweitzer. Hylton's closest rival in showmanship was Jack Payne, whose years as conductor of the BBC Dance Orchestra provided him with a custom-built audience when he left the Corporation in 1932 to go on the halls. In his biography *Signature Tune*, Payne described how stunt had to follow stunt, and stage band leaders had to build their acts into such enormous shows that it was almost impossible to keep up with them. Payne found himself riding elephants and flying aeroplanes (he had been an RFC pilot in World War I) for films which could be back-projected on stage while the band played appropriate numbers. He and Hylton, with other leaders such as Lew Stone, became involved in off-stage publicity junkets, but it was all part and parcel of the show business of which musicians now found themselves such a vital part. Hylton even put out a fifteen-piece band fronted by his wife Ennis, and I recall, as a boy, seeing Mrs Jack Hylton and her Band at the Queen's Theatre in South Shields. The band comedian was a young man who rushed round the stalls distributing pictures of himself with the verbal introduction 'Trinder's the name—you lucky people!' Decades later Tommy Trinder was one of Britain's leading comics topping the bill at the London Palladium; and still doing the same act.

Both Harry Roy and Billy Cotton were originally conventional dance band leaders whose natural flair for comedy stood them in good stead when they took to the stage. Roy's band show bordered on madness, but unlike other comedy bands of the thirties and forties like Syd Seymour and his Mad Hatters, Dr Crock and his Crackpots and Sid Millward and the Nitwits, Harry Roy retained a degree of musical sophistication despite the comedy work of singer Bill Currie, drummer Joe Daniels (replaced by Ray Ellington), saxist Abe Romaine, pianists Ivor Moreton and Dave Kaye *et al*. Billy Cotton's stage act inclined more towards the vaudeville tradition. Singer Alan Breeze was a versatile performer in sketches along with Cotton, who was never merely a front man, and one of the highlights of the show was the tap dancing of veteran Negro trombonist Ellis Jackson. The *Billy Cotton Band Show* was less a dance band than a music hall attraction, and when theatres closed all over the country in the fifties it became one of the BBC's top television and radio programmes until Cotton's death in 1969. The only attempt at musical humour in recent years was by the Temperance Seven, an unfunny band specialising in deadpan interpretations of 1920s style arrangements of songs of that era.

Generally speaking, American bands eschewed the more extrovert forms of comedy, although Milt Britton and his band did an act (seen briefly in the 1943 film *Melody Inn*) that was sheer slapstick. That same year studio drummer Lindley A. 'Spike' Jones assembled some of his fellow session men for a record of 'Der Fuehrer's Face', a Disney cartoon song, giving it the full corny treatment. It was such a success that Spike Jones and his City Slickers became a full-time comedy act, appearing on stage and in films, and making a series of records of such unlikely songs as 'Laura', 'Cocktails For Two' and 'Chloe' in which the lyrics were parodied by comic sound effects and exaggerations of musical style. It was incredibly well done, the split-second timing and grade A musicianship lending a validity to performances that are still funny today. In the mid-forties one of Spike's sidemen, former Ted Weems saxophonist Red Ingle, branched out with his Natural Seven, whose cod hillbilly playing (plus singing by Jo Stafford, revealing an unexpected flair for satire as vocalist Cinderella G. Stump) was wickedly accurate. Also it was prophetic—Ingle's deliberate simplification of the harmonies of 'Temptation' was no funnier than the unintentionally banal version of the song by the Everly Brothers a decade later.

Possibly the earliest show band, even pre-Whiteman, was Fred Waring and his Pennsylvanians. Starting as a collegiate band at Penn State College under singer Tom Waring's direction, it was expanded by brother Fred into a full-scale orchestra which at first did comedy numbers and routines. Fred Waring eventually developed the vocal team—including embryo film stars Lola, Rosemary and Priscilla Lane, actress-authoress Kay

Fred Waring's Pennsylvanians were America's No 1 orchestral-choral organisation for many decades.

Ina Ray Hutton and her Melodears in *The Big Broadcast of 1936*. Pianist Ruth Lowe later wrote two Sinatra hits, 'I'll Never Smile Again' and 'Put Your Dreams Away'. (*Paramount Pictures*)

Thompson and choral director Robert Shaw—into the magnificent Glee Club which was a prototype for choirs all over the States served by Waring arrangements and publications. During World War II Fred Waring opened his Broadway headquarters every Wednesday evening to servicemen in New York, the hospitality including supper at which boys and girls from the neighbouring theatres mingled with the servicemen, the later part of the evening being devoted to a concert in Waring's enormous rehearsal room in which the full orchestra and Glee Club took part. Fred Waring himself was a table-tennis nut who offered to take on anyone from among the onlookers. Just for the record, I lost, 21–3!

Obviously all-girl bands would be a natural visual attraction, and if they got by on looks rather than musicianship, well, that was their prerogative. Few achieved any sort of prominence, probably for this reason, but the best and most durable was Ina Ray Hutton and her Melodears. Ina Ray, elder sister of Pied Pipers singer June Hutton, was just eighteen and dancing in *The Ziegfeld Follies* when she formed her first band in 1934. In a way she combined the two careers, for her sinuous weaving that replaced orthodox con-ducting was the band's principal selling point to a male audience. But by 1940 even the leader had tired of the all-girl bit and with tenor sax-arranger George Paxton as musical boss of the outfit she weaved in front of a conventional dance band, only returning to the all-girl formula years later when television provided a showcase that lasted for four years. The other girl band show that attracted a great public was Phil Spitalny and his Hour Of Charm, featuring Evelyn and her Magic Violin. Oddly enough, although Spitalny's twenty-five piece orchestra was loaded with visual appeal, its attractions went unseen on radio; equally odd was his decision not to take advantage of television as did Ina Ray Hutton. At a time when his pulchritudinous personnel could have been seen coast to coast, Spitalny married his Magic Violinist and retired to Miami Beach where he filled in time as a music critic on the local paper. Britain's only comparable band was given the biggest possible send-off during World War II when the BBC appointed Ivy Benson and her All-Girls' Band as their official dance band, a decision that caused no little bitchiness in the profession, it being felt that the girls' talent was hardly comparable to that of the many good bands which would have welcomed such an appointment. However, Ivy survived and was a major attraction for many years after leaving the BBC.

The most prominent American show bands were Horace Heidt and his Musical Knights, Kay Kyser and his College Of Musical Knowledge and Sammy Kaye and his band, whose slogan was 'swing and sway with Sammy Kaye'. Heidt's band was never a particularly good one although it included at various times people like Frank De Vol, Frankie Carle, Al Hirt and Alvino Rey, later to become leaders of note; but its musical value became secondary to the presentation of such gimmick shows as *Answers By The Dancers*, *Youth Opportunity*, *Anniversary Night*, *Treasure Chest* and *Pot O' Gold*, one of the earliest give-away radio shows. Like Heidt, Kay Kyser favoured the Guy Lombardo approach with cloying saxes and staccato brass, but here again the musical shortcomings took second place to the quiz that gave the outfit its name. Kyser took the band into films in 1939 with some success, and in the mid-forties developed a more progressive musical policy. Of the three, Kaye followed most closely the Lombardo style and adopted Kyser's musical signature of 'singing songtitles' (so did Blue Barron), in which each song was introduced by a vocalist singing the title line before the arrangement began. His audience participation gimmick was 'So You Want To Lead A Band' in which dancers, or members of a theatre or TV audience, competed for prizes by conducting the band. When Kaye went into television he also ensured a modicum of respect from music lovers by improving the standard of his music. But, on the whole, television wasn't much help to big bands, even those dedicated to show-

Former polka band leader, accordion-playing **Lawrence Welk** was one of the few leaders to make a successful career on television. (*Pye Records*)

manship. Heidt, Kaye and Kyser never equalled their radio success, nor did most others who tried.

Comedian Jackie Gleason, television's top performer of the early fifties and a lifelong devotee of big bands, featured many of them on his show over the years and at one time had Paul Whiteman as MC introducing four different bands each week. His greatest contribution to the cause was to provide a regular showcase for the Dorsey Brothers Orchestra, a long stint ended only by the deaths of the brothers within seven months of each other. After that there was only Lawrence Welk and his Champagne Music Makers whose show started from the Aragon Ballroom in Santa Monica in 1952 and just ran and ran and ran. With thirty musicians and thirteen singers it soon outgrew the ballroom and occupied all available studio space. Led by Scandinavian farm boy Welk (born in 1903 and a polka band leader since 1925) on accordion with champagne bubbles rampant through the music, it was hardly the big band sound as we knew it. But it gave employment to musicians long after the Big Band Era had faded and reminded the public at large that band music of a kind wasn't quite dead.

Society Style

Society style music was known in the trade as 'mickey mouse music'. Guy Lombardo and his Royal Canadians were the archetype, the father and mother, the patron saint and guardian angel of all mickey mouse bands. It was actually a family co-operative unit run by the Lombardo brothers, Guy, Carmen, Lebert and Victor (sister Rosemarie also sang

Eddy Duchin and his Orchestra, the archetypal piano-led society band of the thirties. (*Paramount Pictures*)

with the band) from London, Ontario. They played for decades at the Roosevelt Grill, New York, and their style changed as little as their location. A 1972 Lombardo record sounds just like a 1932 Lombardo record, with the gutless, simpering saxophones led by Carmen's wide vibrato, corny brass playing (Lebert was in charge of that), tinkling twin pianos and a beatless 'rhythm' section. (No, that's not quite fair—they did swop banjo and sousaphone for guitar and bass somewhere along the line, but it's hard to tell aurally just when the change took place.)

I saw Lombardo on stage at Loew's State Theatre on Broadway supporting an MGM musical *Thrill Of A Romance* which wound up with a fine flourish from the mighty Tommy Dorsey band, filling the theatre with sound. Then the curtains parted and there was this tinny little band trying to fill an enormous theatre—the contrast was just too much. But give Lombardo credit; he found a style and stuck to it. To some of us it may not have been a good style, but it was his own, dancers loved it and Guy is probably the world's richest bandleader. So mark him down as an original, also an influence, for his stylistic simplicity was plagiarised by not only the less significant society bands but many bigger names. To those of Heidt, Kyser and Kaye must also be added Jan Garber ('the idol of the air lanes'), Blue Barron and, in particular, British maestro Maurice Winnick who adopted not only a carbon copy of the Lombardo style but also Guy's slogan 'The Sweetest Music This Side Of Heaven' as his own theme song.

Society's favourite music was that of the piano-playing bandleader of which Eddie Duchin was the prototype, with melodic but flashy piano backed by tenor-led saxes and muted trumpet, the whole played at the sort of tempo known as 'business men's bounce'. Duchin's former twin-pianist in the Leo Reisman band, Nat Brandwynne, Jack Fina, Henry King, Joe Reichman, Ted Straeter, Barclay Allen, and (for my money the best of them) Carmen Cavallaro, all led dance bands which seldom hit the highspots or became household names but which found steady employment in the most select locations. Like Vincent Lopez who was at the Taft Hotel in New York for years. One of the most distinguished hotel bands was that of Johnny Green, better known as composer of such standards as 'Body And Soul', 'Out Of Nowhere' and 'I Cover The Waterfront' and as musical director for many MGM musicals of the forties and fifties. Green (who recorded with Fred Astaire in the mid-thirties) had a good band well served by his own musicianly but never over-ambitious scores and, not its least attraction, his own elegant piano playing.

More subtle than that of the average café pianist, and nicely phrased with just enough syncopation to avoid being corny, Green's style was not unlike that of his good friend, Massachusetts-born Carroll Gibbons who led the Savoy Orpheans in London for so many years. After Gibbons's death in 1954 the Savoy Hotel's music was in the hands of his former deputy pianist Ian Stewart, who made more of a name as a recording pianist than as a bandleader. His general style was less akin to that of Gibbons than to Charlie Kunz, leader of an undistinguished band at the Casani Club before the war, but more famed for his recorded piano medleys which must have sold millions over two decades thanks to the simple, corny style which presented the hits of the day just as the public liked to hear them. Like Gibbons and Pennsylvanian Kunz, Jack Harris arrived in London from America in the twenties, and although not a high-ranking name on either side of the Atlantic he did have an efficient hotel and night club band before returning to the States on the outbreak of war. Others of that era were Al Collins at the Berkeley Hotel and Bram Martin at the Holborn Restaurant, both of whom, as string players, proved that old bandleaders never die—they wind up as session men in the lucrative recording and film business of today. Noel 'Chappie' D'Amato, Jack Hylton's guitarist, played for a time with Jack Jackson when

Jack Harris and his Orchestra in the studio for one of the stylish recordings (many with Sid Phillips arrangements) made in 1937–9. (*World Records*)

he too left Hylton, and was later musical director at Hatchette's Restaurant in Piccadilly, his most memorable music being created during the war when Hatchette's Swingtette featured Stephane Grappelly and Arthur Young. Pianist Eddie Carroll at the Empress Rooms, violinists Sydney Kyte at the Piccadilly Hotel and Brian Lawrence at Quaglino's Restaurant and Lansdowne House, the American Starita brothers, Al, Ray and Rudy, at various West End spots—these were the darlings of London's society crowd between the wars. Things were never quite the same when peace returned, although Jack Nathan and Ronnie Pleydell both had bands a cut above the usual society style and Felix King made Cavallaro-inspired sounds at the Nightingale. But the newly minted title of 'deb's delight' was shared by Paul Adam and Tommy Kinsman, both of whom broadcast and recorded frequently but who must have earned the greater part of their incomes from society engagements.

Leo Reisman and his Orchestra. Here Leo Reisman gets a 'bon voyage' from Guatemalan Consul General Gustavo Rivas, on leaving to play at Guatemala Fair and President's Reception. (The giant hot-dog is to depict the most typical U.S. food). (*RCA Records, New York*)

Their counterparts in American society included Meyer Davis, Ernie Hecksher, Lester Lanin, Emil Coleman, Ben Selvin, and others who were mentioned at the outset as being in the vanguard of organised dance music. For decades these men provided bands for society gigs, all playing the same ultra-sophisticated, eager beaver, business men's bounce. No tricky scores, just lush unison playing that suited the dancers as well as the rota of free-lance musicians who flitted in and out of the bands from one gig to another. One of the busier contractors like Lanin or Davis could have up to fifty bands operating under his name in one night. Johnny Green proved that society style wasn't always synonymous with mickey mouse music, as did the bands of Gus Arnheim, Ted Fio Rito and Abe Lyman, all equally well-known as songwriters. Lyman and Arnheim began as joint leaders of the Syncopated Five in the Roaring Twenties, at which time they collaborated in writing 'I Cried For You'. After they split Arnheim made a name for himself at the Cocoanut Grove in Hollywood; and not merely because his vocalists around 1931–2 were successively Bing Crosby and Russ Columbo. RCA have frequently reissued Bing's recordings of that era and it's my view at least that the Arnheim sides stand the test of time better than Crosby's sides with Whiteman. Later in the thirties Arnheim discarded his society image and adopted a swing style partly based on arrangements by his twenty-five year old pianist Stan Kenton. Lyman also had a good band which at various times included legendary jazz harpist Caspar Reardon and guitarist Teddy Powell, who went on to become a swing band leader and a prolific songwriter. Ted Fio Rito set a standard above the norm for society and hotel music. In between writing such songs as 'I Never Knew', 'Toot Toot Tootsie Goodbye' and 'Laugh Clown Laugh' his polished arrangements not only pleased dancers at Chicago's Edgewater Beach Hotel but served as a backdrop for young singers Betty Grable and Leif Ericson who had other things to do in later years. Other famous names in embryo were found in the ranks of Anson Weeks's band at the Mark Hopkins Hotel in San Francisco, like violinist Xavier Cugat, saxophonist-singer Tony Martin and vocalists Bob Crosby and Dale Evans, all of whom entertained Californian society.

One could say that what Weeks was to the West Coast Leo Reisman was to the East.

Freddie Martin and his Orchestra run through a new score at an RCA Victor session. Another posthumous hit for Tchaikovsky or Grieg? (*RCA Records, New York*)

Certainly the former violinist with the Baltimore Symphony was not only successful at his job of playing for New York's élite at the Waldorf-Astoria and the Central Park Casino. He had a highly competent musical organisation which recorded with Lee Wiley, Harold Arlen and Fred Astaire, with whom Reisman did the Original Cast album of the 1931 show *Band Wagon*, as well as a number of historic recordings in which Astaire appeared in the role of band vocalist rather than as the star. But to me the best society band of all was Freddie Martin's. Basically it ran true to form with tenor lead, muted trumpets, a flavouring of fiddles and strict adherence to the melody, but what set it apart was not only the well-controlled approach to sweet music but also the warm, mellow tone imparted to the ensemble by the lead tenor Freddie Martin himself. His playing was strictly non-jazz, a perfectly academic tenor saxophone sound that matched the sort of ensemble he led, yet George T. Simon has revealed how jazz saxists like Johnny Hodges, Chu Berry and Eddie Miller revered Martin's tone. Resident at the Cocoanut Grove, Martin sold himself to record buyers in 1942 with his hit version of part of Tchaikovsky's Piano Concerto No 1 in B flat minor, under the title 'Tonight We Love', the first of many similar classics in dance tempo. While playing his Music In The Martin Manner at the St Regis Roof in New York Martin was featuring Russ Morgan on piano and trombone, and it was hardly coincidence that when Morgan left to form his own band in 1935 he called it Music In The Morgan Manner, adopting a reasonable facsimile of the Martin sound, even to his own trombone 'wha-wah' interjections which had been Martin's trademark. From then until the end of the Big Band Era no one had a keener sense of public taste, so much so that by 1949 his was one of the few bands to make the Top Twenty. On one occasion he had four records in the charts including his own famous song 'So Tired'. (He also wrote his theme song 'Does Your Heart Beat For Me', 'You're Nobody Till Somebody Loves You' and other potboilers.)

Formerly arranger for Sousa and Victor Herbert and a member of the Detroit Symphony, Russ Morgan was equally well-versed in the sort of jazz that was never allowed to creep into his own band, having scored for the Jean Goldkette band and played trombone with a

Gray Gordon, another 'mickey mouse' leader (a metronomic 'Tic-Toc Rhythm' was his gimmick) also went into artists management. (*RCA Records, New York*)

1935 revival of the Original Dixieland Jazz Band, the same year he recorded a set of violin-piano duets with Joe Venuti. All this was subordinated to the business of pleasing the people. Successfully, I might add, for Morgan's was one of the most consistent sweet bands, one that teetered on the edge of the mickey mouse style but never embraced it completely. Among those who did, and reflected the fact in their titles, were Art Kassell and his Kassells In The Air, Enoch Light and the Light Brigade, Gray Gordon and his Tic-Toc Rhythm, and Shep Fields and his Rippling Rhythm. I never minded Shep's band. It had a not unattractive sound despite the gimmick of introducing each tune by blowing into a glass of water through a straw. This was the prelude to a rippling effect suggested by the scoring for woodwinds, accordion and viola, an overall effect that was quite pleasing—certainly more so than Lawrence Welk's champagne bubbles a couple of decades later. In the early forties Fields tired of rippling and went to the other extreme with a big band featuring ten saxophones which, when I saw it in 1945, produced one of the most thrilling and sonorous ensembles I had ever heard, only to be surpassed a year or two later when George Evans (who, strangely enough, never heard the Fields band until I played him some of its records in 1949) came up with a similar but more swinging band in Britain.

Master of 'Rippling Rhythm' in the thirties, **Shep Fields** had a first-class all-saxophone band in the forties and now functions as manager of show business stars like Phil Silvers and Fred Astaire.

Palais Style

'Palais bands' were a phenomenon peculiar to Britain. America had its share of run-of-the-mill ballroom bands but only in Britain did they achieve any sort of national prominence. And most assuredly were American listeners spared the metronomical strict tempo music which formed a large part of British dance music due to the tremendous interest in formal ballroom dancing, a favourite pursuit of those who neither know nor care anything about music but insist that a foxtrot must be played at 32 bars per minute and a quickstep at 48, otherwise their twinkling little toes are incapable of functioning properly. This fanaticism

Victor Silvester, top-ranking
strict tempo maestro for over forty
years. (*EMI Records*)

was carried over from championship events into ordinary local hops, and while fronting a semi-pro band I often had some pompous idiot coming up to the stand, stop-watch in hand, and complaining because the band was playing at 31½ or 49bpm. To spare these earnest souls the agony of minuscule variations in their travelling speed various dancing teachers lent their names to recordings produced for use in dance studios and ballrooms. The high priest of strict tempo is Victor Silvester, a former champion dancer who supervised his first strict tempo records in 1934, since when his Ballroom Orchestra must have recorded, broadcast and televised more than any other band in the world. The line-up was violin, alto sax and a metronomical rhythm section, with little variation in the 'arrangements'; but recently Silvester has added four other saxes and even, on occasion, such madly contemporary touches as electric organ and guitar. The skeletal format was followed by other non-conducting dance teacher-'leaders' like Wally Fryer, Josephine Bradley and Norman Grant, and at one time was even adopted by Joe Loss and Oscar Rabin for special strict tempo recordings. Functional dance records are still being made by bands like those of Ray McVay and Charles Barlow who realise that today's ballroom dancers like something a little more interesting musically, even if the result is little more than Glenn Miller-and-water. Old-time dancing has always had its adherents and interpreters, though how long it will be before the quickstep, waltz and foxtrot are relegated to this category is anybody's guess. The prime mover was Harry Davidson, a light orchestral conductor who, at the instigation of Fred Hartley, the BBC's Director Of Light Music in the forties, included old-time dances in his programmes and eventually did all his broadcasts and recordings in this idiom, being followed on the market by Sidney Bowman and Sydney Thompson, who now has his own record company specialising in old-time dance music.

'Palais de danse' was a generic term used in Britain to describe any public dancing spot from London's converted Lyceum Theatre and Hammersmith Palais to the tattiest provincial barn, but whatever the ambience, the palais was not so much a recreation for the young people of Britain as a way of life. A release of tension in wartime, a social centre in peacetime, and an informal marriage bureau at all times. How many thousands of married couples must have first met and courted beneath the revolving crystal ball of the local palais? For them, and others like myself who only went to hear the guest bands, dance music and the tunes of the day inevitably have personal associations, either of romance or of a form of musical entertainment now gone forever. Like the great American ballrooms the British palais were the centres of operations for the big bands on one-night stands. They were the gods, the almighty visitors who descended for one evening and were as quickly gone. But night after night, week after week, the palais had their own resident bands, often on a part-time basis, workmanlike bands who never scaled the heights. Their budgets did not allow for special arrangements and they relied on publishers' stocks, so that on any one night you could walk into a palais anywhere in Britain and hear the same

Billy Merrin and his Commanders made the Nottingham Palais de Danse a well-known provincial dance spot. (*Memory Lane*)

arrangements, be they the current pops or the carbon copy scores of 'In The Mood', 'Skyliner' or 'Hors d'oeuvres', the only difference being in the standard of performance. This in turn depended on the stature of the palais and its band rather than on the musical appreciation of the dancers. Nevertheless, many palais bands had their followers, especially those lucky enough to be resident at halls wired for outside broadcasts, or which were of a high enough standard to meet the BBC's stringent requirements for studio broadcasts. Harry Leader and Jack White at the Astoria, Ken Mackintosh at the Empire, Lou Preager and Phil Tate at Hammersmith Palais, Ivor Kirchin at the Lyceum were among the principal London palais bands along with men like Nat Allen, David Ede and Joe Loss who, despite the fame he achieved during a forty-five year career, always had the archetypal palais band.

But although London is the centre of British music, some provincial bands achieved wider popularity and managed to bring a fairly high standard of music to the 80 per cent of Britain's population living outside the capital. There was Syd Dean in Brighton, Johnny Rosen in Manchester, Billy Merrin and his Commanders in Nottingham, Bertini and Larry Brennan at the Tower Ballroom in Blackpool where Charles Barlow now holds sway, and Peter Fielding at the Oxford Galleries in Newcastle, succeeded in the early fifties by George Evans, who took his excellent big band with its ten saxophones off the road in favour of a long-term residency. It's also worth noting that two of the few bands left in Britain today originated in and operate from Manchester, where the BBC formed its Northern Dance Orchestra under Alyn Ainsworth's expert direction in the mid-fifties. Bernard Herrmann now conducts the NDO, no longer a mere utility orchestra but a first-class working band. It was while with the NDO that trumpeter Syd Lawrence started a spare-time rehearsal band of local musicians playing old Glenn Miller arrangements, one that grew so popular with local listeners that he finally put the band on a professional footing and is now one of the busiest leaders in the country with broadcasts, recordings and personal appearances.

And Some of That Jazz

Although jazz *per se* is outside the scope of this book, as a separate musical world already more than adequately documented, a number of jazz (or neo-jazz) bands have crossed the borderlines of popular music. It has even been known for jazz records to earn Gold Discs for sales of a million records, a process that began in 1927 when Red Nichols and his Five Pennies recorded 'Ida', and was still going on in 1961 with the Dave Brubeck Quartet's 'Take Five', a year later with Stan Getz and Charlie Byrd's 'Desafinado' and in 1965 with the Ramsey Lewis Trio's 'The In Crowd'. So jazz presented in a form acceptable to the masses can be a commercial proposition, sometimes even without making the concessions to public taste that Louis Armstrong did with 'Hello Dolly' and 'What A Wonderful World' in the sixties.

The one jazzman universally known was Thomas 'Fats' Waller, whose seemingly endless series of recordings with His Rhythm always managed to combine good jazz (Waller's own marvellously swinging stride piano allied to spirited ensemble work from trumpeter Herman Autrey and clarinettist Gene Sedric) with sound commercial appeal, even if his satirical performance of some abysmal songs wasn't always recognised as such. Waller is by no means out of place here, for as well as recording with the bands of Ted Lewis (1931), Jack Teagarden (1931), McKinney's Cotton Pickers (1929) and the Blue Rhythm Band (1932), he also had his own big band on several occasions between 1935 and 1942. Wingie Manone and his little band came over to our side of the fence with a still-remembered version of 'The Isle Of Capri' that did wonders for that schmaltzy ballad, Bob Howard and his band had a minor hit with 'Throwing Stones At The Sun', and the Riley-Farley Onyx Club Boys gave the world a new catch phrase about the same time (1935) with 'The Music Goes Round And Around'. They never had another hit but found plenty of work on the strength of that one, recording under such names as Ted Russell's Orchestra, The Top Hatters and, with Red McKenzie, founder of the band, as The Rhythm Kings.

All these bands were playing typical 52nd Street swing of the mid-thirties, but two prominent musicians who made attempts to introduce unorthodox voicings to small group

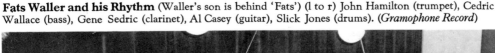

Fats Waller and his Rhythm (Waller's son is behind 'Fats') (l to r) John Hamilton (trumpet), Cedric Wallace (bass), Gene Sedric (clarinet), Al Casey (guitar), Slick Jones (drums). (*Gramophone Record*)

Raymond Scott and his Quintet
(l to r) Johnny Williams (drums), Dave
Wade (trumpet), Raymond Scott
(piano), Dave Harris (tenor), Lou
Shoobe (bass), Pete Pumiglio (clarinet).

music deserved greater success than they achieved. Composer-arranger Alec Wilder started experimenting with new ideas on a Mildred Bailey recording session which he was scoring and directing, and in 1939 expanded the results into the Alec Wilder Octet, combining modern rhythms with harpsichord and neo-baroque scoring for the sort of woodwinds (oboe, cor anglais, bass clarinet etc) not normally heard in dance music. A man of urbane wit, Wilder gave his compositions such inventive titles as 'Neurotic Goldfish', 'Amorous Poltergeist', 'Bull Fiddles In A China Shop' and 'Jack, This Is My Husband'. The Wilder Octets were one of the truly new sounds in—what? Was it jazz, dance music, swing, popular classics—or just plain music? But even Alec could hardly match some of the titles Raymond Scott gave to the pieces he wrote for his Quintet. 'Toy Trumpet' and 'In An Eighteenth Century Drawing Room' are harmless and familiar, but what about 'Dinner Music For A Pack Of Hungry Cannibals', 'War Dance For Wooden Indians' or—wait for it—'Dedicatory Piece To The Crew And Passengers Of The First Experimental Rocket Express To The Moon'? Scott used more orthodox instrumentation than Wilder, but this invited comparison with the better-known swing groups, and once the novelty of his eccentric writing wore off the lack of any rhythmic impulse became evident. But Raymond Scott more than compensated in the forties when he organised a big band that played beautifully his larger-scale orchestrations in swing style. Yet it's still the Raymond Scott Quintet and those oddly titled and odd sounding pieces that people remember, so in retrospect perhaps his contribution was greater than we realised.

In the mid-forties pianist Eddie Heywood's small band with Vic Dickenson on trombone and Doc Cheatham on trumpet had a hit with 'Begin The Beguine', and at the same time Louis Jordan's Tympani Five, first organised in 1939, began to be noticed with 'Is You Is Or Is You Ain't My Baby', 'Beware' and other rocking titles that presaged the eventual take over of the music scene by rhythm and blues. In the postwar years Earl Bostic coarsened the tone of his alto sax and turned his version of 'Flamingo' into a standard, tenor player Charlie Ventura left Gene Krupa and formed his own 'bop for the people' band, but the most commercially successful jazzman of the fifties turned out to be Londoner George Shearing who went to the States just after the war to make his fortune and did just that with a quintet formula, first heard in 'September In The Rain', in which his locked-hands style piano combined in block chords with vibes and guitar, phrasing slightly behind the beat. It was a unique and instantly successful formula and it was over twenty years before the blind pianist could rid himself of his image as a superior cocktail pianist. Meanwhile, however, the Shearing Quintet combined with big bands, string orchestras and singers like Peggy Lee and Nat King Cole; and if George Shearing was no longer regarded with affection by the jazz cognoscenti he at least became one of the few jazzmen to make the music commercially acceptable, in however diluted a form. So did former Cab Calloway trumpeter

Former Casa Loma trombonist **Pee Wee Hunt** had a surprise hit in 1948 with his band's 'cod' version of 'Twelfth Street Rag'. (*Capitol Records*)

Louis Armstrong All Stars in concert; Trummy Young (trombone); Louis Armstrong (trumpet); Edmond Hall (clarinet); Barrett Deems (drums); Arvell Shaw (bass). (*Kenneth Pitt*)

Jonah Jones in the late fifties when his tightly muted horn with rhythm backing produced some superbly swinging music that had all the spirit of true jazz yet also made the Jonah Jones Quartet as big an in-person attraction as it was on records.

Around 1954–5 the onset of rock and roll was answered, as if in protest by more conservative musicians and fans, by a worldwide revival of the traditional jazz style. This doesn't concern us too much here, save as an indication that while big bands were dying all over the place the music which had been popular in their early days was not out of favour. Little of the revivalist stuff was worth much, commercially inspired as it was. Some of it may have been born out of a genuine affection for the music by the players concerned, but this was not reflected by any marked ability to play in any other than a forced pedestrian style which bore only the most superficial resemblance to real New Orleans jazz. But it was popular, and outrageously uniformed bands proved real crowd-pullers. In the club atmosphere where critical faculties tend to be suspended some of it probably sounded quite effective. It was when trad jazz got on to record that its deficiencies were cruelly exposed. All the bands trying to play this essentially black music were white, most of them young men who had no first-hand experience of the music they were aping. The revival started on the West Coast with Turk Murphy, Lu Watters and Bob Scobey in San Francisco and the Firehouse Five + Two in Hollywood, although in fact it had been anticipated a year or two earlier in 1948, when an amusing send-up of the Dixieland style in '12th Street Rag' by former Casa Loma trombonist Pee Wee Hunt and his band had done well and probably conned unknowing listeners into believing that this was the real thing. The Dukes Of Dixieland at least had the honour of recording with Louis Armstrong, which raised the standard of their performance somewhat, but the best Dixieland of the era came from the Lawson-Haggart Jazz Band and Matty Matlock's Dixielanders. Both bands were highly professional, consisting of sidemen from the big band days, including the leaders and others from the old Bob Crosby band, which had always specialised in this idiom. Some of Yank Lawson and Bob Haggart's men stayed with them in the seventies as The World's Greatest Jazz Band which proved that white-haired but still energetic jazz was still very much alive.

The revivalist craze spread to Britain where, as 'trad', a multitude of sins were committed in its name. Chief among the protagonists were the bands of Acker Bilk, Chris Barber, Kenny Ball, Terry Lightfoot, Cy Laurie, Alex Welsh, Humphrey Lyttelton, Freddie Randall and Mick Mulligan. Whatever ideas or feeling the bands may have had were negated by their insistence on recreating the old New Orleans bands right down to the banjos and soggy rhythm sections, and for the most part the music was purely mechanical. But then Britain never did have a jazz tradition. There had been bands which took their music seriously, like George Webb's Dixielanders who were as righteous as one would expect a British semi-pro band to be in 1945, the Vic Lewis-Jack Parnell Jazzmen formed while the leaders were on RAF service in 1944, and Harry Gold and his Pieces Of Eight (which included future orchestral conductors Norrie Paramor, Geoff Love and Ron Goodwin). In prewar years there had been attempts at small group swing by George Scott-Wood and his Six Swingers; Billy Mason's 1935 band, two of whose members, tenor Buddy

What little British jazz there was in the thirties was provided by **Nat Gonella and his Georgians.** Nat Gonella in action at the Empire Theatre, Leeds, in 1935, with Don Barrigo (tenor); Bob Dryden (drums); Tiny Winters (bass); Monia Liter (piano). (*Alan Kane*)

Featherstonhaugh and trumpeter Duncan Whyte, later had their own jazz dance bands; Johnnie Claes and his Clae-Pigeons; and Joe Daniels and his Hot Shots, but these now sound dated and devoid of any real swing. The most durable 'hot' music in Britain was provided (prewar) by Nat Gonella and his Georgians and (postwar) by Sid Phillips and his band, both of which operated as dance bands but never neglected the basics of jazz. Gonella, star trumpet soloist with the bands of Billy Cotton, Roy Fox, Lew Stone and others, was an unashamed copyist of Louis Armstrong, even singing in a pastiche of the Satchmo style. But he was honest about it and we accepted him because he did it well, and from 1934 till his war service, Gonella's Georgians were a top stage and radio attraction. He never regained his former status after the war but is still playing. Sid Phillips was a multi-talented man who preceded and survived the trad boom. His arrangements were responsible for the success of the Ambrose band in the early thirties and when he formed his own little band in 1946 (it lasted over a quarter of a century until his death in 1973) he played and arranged an idiosyncratic type of Dixieland built around his own clarinet. The other British groups which survived did so by adopting a more free-wheeling, mainstream jazz style.

The bebop craze circa 1947 made its mark on British music although not with any great commercial rewards. Tito Burns's Sextet was based on Charlie Ventura's 'bop for the people' group but introduced a number of future bandleading talents including Johnny Dankworth, whose Dankworth Seven turned into the big band mentioned in Chapter 5. Norman Burns copied the Shearing formula, and while altoist Harry Hayes was undoubtedly influenced by Johnny Hodges, his 1946 band produced some pleasant and reasonably original music. When the bop era ended there were a number of modern jazz groups resident at London clubs but these made little impact outside jazz circles.

This 1949 one night stand by the **Tito Burns Band** at the Southall Swing Club recalls those exciting days of British bebop when future reputations were being made by (l to r) Tito Burns, Cab Kaye, Dennis Rose, Ronnie Scott, Johnny Dankworth, Tony Crombie, Joe Muddell and Bernie Fenton. (*Kenneth Pitt*)

Exotica

Latin-American and Hawaiian music were always popular offshoots from dance music's main stem, though both were inevitably offered to the public in watered down form. As the new Latin dances were introduced in each era (the tango in the twenties, rumba in the thirties, conga and samba in the forties, mambo and cha-cha-cha in the fifties and bossa

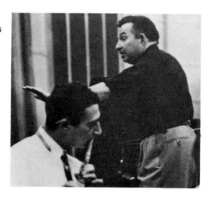

The chihuahua and casual air were for the public. This shot from an RCA Victor recording session shows **Xavier Cugat** as a far from casual conductor. (*RCA Records, New York*)

nova in the sixties), so the bands specialising in the rhythms had their moment of glory. The tango, glamorised by Rudolf Valentino, was handled better by light orchestras, but in 1930 Geraldo and his Gaucho Tango Orchestra did so well in broadcasts and stage shows and at the Savoy Hotel in London, that Londoner Gerald Bright was known in Britain as the 'tango king', although his 'gauchos' (and their music) were about as authentic as Geraldo himself. Venetian-born violinist Annunzio P. Mantovani also went in for spurious exotica with his Tipica Orchestra featuring accordionist Ronald Binge. After a spell of conventional dance band leading, Mantovani and Binge formulated a new string sound for a recording of 'Charmaine' which launched the former Tipica leader as an important world figure in the field of lush mood music. Two of the more authentic Latin bands from Cuba were those of Don Azpiazu and composer Ernesto Lecuona, and if their music was probably as commercially angled as that of any other Latin band there was a sort of ethnic purity about it that made it more acceptable to aficionados. Most successful of all was Xavier Cugat, for reasons specified in Chapter 7 on bands in films. Many years' residence at the Waldorf-Astoria in New York made Cugat the Latin showman supreme, and his music was almost symphonic in style—you could call him the Paul Whiteman of Latin music— but quite splendid with good brass and saxes, sensuous strings, melodious marimbas and its undoubtedly rhythmic percussion section, one of whose members, Desi Arnaz, left to form

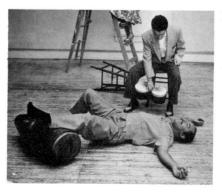

Perez Prado, whose big brass and percussion made the mambo the big craze of the early fifties. (*RCA Records, New York*)

his own Latin dance band before finding TV fame as actor and comedian with his then wife Lucille Ball. Bandleading alone would never have given Arnaz the power to buy up the RKO film studios and set up Desilu Productions. Cugat's ex-vocalist Miguelito Valdes, Enric Madriguera and Chuy Reyes had society bands with the accent on Latin rhythms, but there were no really new sounds or rhythms until 1950 when Perez Prado popularised the mambo.

Roberto Inglez, the Savoy Hotel's master of soothing Latin rhythms. (*EMI Records*)

The former pianist-arranger with the Orquesta Casino De La Playa had been fascinated by the mambo as far back as 1943, and although it was introduced in Mexico by the bands of Anselmo Sacasas and Julio Gutierrez, it was Prado who really made it big. He made Mexico City his base and there recorded his own arrangements and compositions (like 'Mambo Jambo' and 'Patricia') for RCA, records which startled the world with their biting brass and emphatic beat, sparked off other similar style bands and gave Latin music a new lease of life. Machito, Tito Rodriguez, Noro Morales, Tito Puente and Rene Touzet may not be names as eminent as Prado's, but they were the backbone of Latin-American music in the fifties. The cha-cha-cha happened along in 1958, but apart from giving Warren Covington and the 'ghost' Tommy Dorsey band a hit with 'Tea For Two Cha-Cha' (and inspiring a few hundred unsuccessful copies based on other standard songs) it didn't mean much. It was a novelty and lacked the rhythmic delicacy of the bossa nova which came up out of Brazil in 1961, gave jazz tenor Stan Getz and guitarist Charlie Byrd a hit with 'Desafinado' and introduced Luiz Bonfa, Joao Gilberto, Eumir Deodato and above all Antonio Carlos Jobim to popular music. Composer of some of the most enchanting melodies ever heard in Latin music, a wonderfully rhythmic guitarist, talented pianist and singer of little ability but plenty of charm, Jobim presented himself admirably on record with large orchestral or small band settings with beautifully complementary scores by Claus Ogerman and Eumir Deodato.

Hardly big band music in the accepted sense, but certainly brassy enough, Herb Alpert's Tijuana Brass adapted the sounds of the Mexican mariachi bands into a commercially acceptable formula. Though the limitations of the style were obvious, the Tijuana Brass was the most popular and influential band sound of the sixties and seventies and set in motion a host of plagiarists. British Latin bands obviously functioned at second or third hand, but produced a pleasant enough sort of commercial dance music with vaguely exotic overtones. Don Marino Barretto was a favourite of the late thirties and early forties, and better known Latin bands of the fifties were those of trumpeter Eddie Calvert and the Hermanos Deniz, a reasonably authentic little band led by guitarists Joe and Frank Deniz. Roberto Inglez (actually Bert Inglis from Scotland) had the relief band at the Savoy Hotel, and about the time that 78rpm records were changing into 45s and LPs he made dozens of

Still going strong, **Edmundo Ros,** Venezuelan-born ex-drummer who formed his first band for London's Cosmo Club in 1940 (Roberto Inglez was his pianist). (*EMI Records*)

very attractive recordings of top Latin tunes, featuring his own single-finger piano (borrowed from Gordon Jenkins) against a mass of strings. But the most popular band for something like thirty years has been that of Edmundo Ros, born in Venezuela in 1910, who once played drums on a Fats Waller session. Ros always had a straight-forward 'no frills' style—block scoring for conventional brass and saxes dance band instrumentation backed by a percussive rhythm section, the very impelling nature of which disarmed criticism.

Hawaiian bands are, on the face of it, a minority interest. But are they? Other musical fashions flash by but every record company has a Hawaiian album or two tucked away in the archives and more are continually being recorded, and presumably sold. So let's not be condescending about it. They are popular and always have been. Hawaiian bands have vanished as far as personal appearances are concerned and most recordings are by session men, but in the thirties and forties Harry Owens (a Nebraskan who got an Academy Award for writing 'Sweet Leilani' and was the most popular bandleader in Hawaii), Andy Iona and his Islanders, Ray Kinney, Lani McIntyre, Roland Peachey, and Felix Mendelssohn and his Hawaiian Serenaders combined languorous music with visual appeal. Latterday groups working in the Islands are those of Martin Denny and Arthur Lyman, who blend traditional Hawaiian music with jazz rhythms and exotic sound effects to make fascinating music a world removed from the steel guitar blandishments of their precursors in the art.

7 HOORAY FOR HOLLYWOOD?

Radio and records may have made dance bands household names but it was left to motion pictures to add the personal touch, the visual image which transformed bandleaders, singers and musicians from disembodied sounds into real personalities. A large proportion of the vast listening and record buying audience had little personal contact with those orchestras holding long-term residencies in hotels and other locations in the major cities. For many fans one-night stands by name bands were few and far between even if a particular town possessed ballrooms or theatres large enough to make a visit by a top musical attraction a financially viable proposition.

But everyone went to the movies, and film makers were quick to realise the drawing power of the big bands, even in purely incidental appearances in night club sequences in non-musical films, and it would be hard to think of a band that didn't feature, however briefly, in such a guest spot at some time in its career. Society bands like those of Gus Arnheim, Abe Lyman, Eddy Duchin, Ted Fio Rito, Will Osborne, Rudy Vallee *et al* made many such appearances during the early thirties, but the first major film to be completely built around a dance band was *The King Of Jazz* in 1930. The advent of the All-Talking All-Singing All-Dancing Era had been the signal for each of the major film studios to mount its own all-star musical extravaganza utilising the services of every contract star on its books. There was *Paramount On Parade*, MGM's *Broadway Melody* and *Hollywood Revue*, and Warners' *On With The Show*, but Universal, though one of the oldest established studios, having been founded by Carl Laemmle in 1912, was still searching for an idea. Until Laemmle's son, as producer, and John Murray Anderson, as director-scenarist, thought of featuring the Paul Whiteman orchestra, at that time America's biggest musical attraction, as the centrepiece of their initial contribution to the genre.

The band left New York for the Coast on a special train hired by Old Gold cigarettes, their radio sponsors, and received a royal welcome at Universal. The event is described in his biography *Call Me Lucky* by Bing Crosby, at that time one of Whiteman's Rhythm Boys:

> We were given a big bungalow on the Universal lot as a recreation room. We all bought autos—or at least we made the down payments with money which Pops advanced to us then deducted from our salaries. We loafed for a month while the big brains worked up a story which proved unsuitable for Whiteman. They made the mistake of trying to build him as a romantic lead. He was impressive looking, but what with his thinning thatch and ample poundage, it was finally decided that he didn't fit the script, so we bundled back into the train and returned to New York.

The film was finally planned as a musical variety show and the band once again headed west. Using new techniques, with the problems of filming in sound and a colour process quite revolutionary for 1930, it developed slowly, meriting the wry Crosby comment that 'We worked on *The King of Jazz* for a coon's age.' It didn't help when Bing earned sixty days without the option on a charge of reckless driving and violating the Prohibition Act. His big solo, 'Song Of The Dawn', went to John Boles, but thanks to Whiteman's intervention Bing was allowed out of jail under escort each day to film the 'Bench In The Park' sequence, a complicated affair involving most of the cast and musicians.

However, *The King Of Jazz* was an enormous success, and although Paul Whiteman quite unjustifiably adopted its title as his own, his future was assured and dance bands found a permanent niche in films, although it was to be some years before Hollywood regarded bandleaders as suitable material for biographical treatment or created any more films around bands rather than treating them purely as background figures. But many of the films, within their limitations, were good showcases for leaders with personality and bands with something to offer musically and visually. Extrovert showman Cab Calloway and his band were featured to advantage in *The Big Broadcast* and other musicals of the thirties, Louis Armstrong made his debut in *Pennies From Heaven* and went on to make over twenty screen appearances in which, perhaps inevitably, his 'mugging' and personality were exploited at the expense of his true jazz talent, while the personable Duke Ellington and his orchestra, after making a 1929 short called *Black and Tan Fantasy*, made their first feature film in the 1930 *Check And Double Check*, following up with *Belle Of The Nineties*, *Murder At The Vanities*, *Cabin In The Sky* and many others. Fred Waring's Pennsylvanians were an outstanding show orchestra, great radio favourites who first starred in the 1929 *Syncopation* and were used extensively as the focal point of Warners' *The Varsity Show* of 1937, the same year in which Benny Goodman and his orchestra starred in *Hollywood Hotel*. (Trumpeter-scat singer-comedian Johnny 'Scat' Davis appeared as a member of both bands, though it is rumoured that Harry James ghosted his playing in the latter film.)

So the regular employment of dance and swing bands continued. Artie Shaw and his orchestra co-starred in *Second Chorus*, conducted in one sequence by a tap-dancing Fred Astaire, while the excellent Paramount production of 1942, *The Fleet's In*, made intelligent use of Jimmy Dorsey's band playing the fine Victor Schertzinger-Johnny Mercer songs. By now it was wartime, with cinema audiences hungry for music, colour, rhythm, and generally escapist entertainment. All the studios concentrated on musicals, even such minor league companies as Republic and Monogram churning out endless streams of B pictures featuring the swing bands of Freddie Slack, Charlie Barnet, Bob Crosby, Louis Jordan, Jack Teagarden, Stan Kenton, Woody Herman etc, along with the popular singers of the day and close harmony groups like the Delta Rhythm Boys, Merry Macs and the Nat King Cole Trio. It was also the day of the 'omnibus' band musical—films like *Reveille With Beverley*, *Jam Session*, *Make Believe Ballroom*, in which studios took advantage of the presence of whatever bands happened to be in Los Angeles at the time to link a series of disconnected musical numbers together by some thin thread of a story, generally involving a disc jockey. At this stage of cinema history, before the double feature became staple fare, there was a huge demand for short films of about ten minutes' duration as programme fillers, and companies specialising in the production of shorts were regular employers of big bands. Some of the films were embarrassingly bad, sometimes the band was relegated to an accompanying role for dull variety acts, but once in a while a creative director could provide fascinating visual imagery by an inventive combination of music and pictures. There were many such series, such as Universal's *Name Band Musicals* of the late forties succeeded by their *Musical Featurettes* of the early fifties. Les Brown, Tex Beneke, Buddy Rich, Gene Krupa, Jimmy and Tommy Dorsey, Duke Ellington, Freddie Martin, Harry James and the Sauter-Finegan Orchestra were just some of the stellar attractions in this series. Other band shorts were featured in such series as *Thrills Of Music*, *Martin Block's Musical Merry-Go-Round*, *Film Vodvil*, *Big Name Bands*, *Movietone Melodies*, *Jamboree*, *Melody Time*; even the notoriously guyed *March Of Time* did occasional jazz editions. The Original Dixieland Jazz Band and others were the subject of one 1937 edition, and Paul Whiteman was honoured twice: with Tommy Dorsey and the Glenn Miller American Air Force Band in 1943; and with Eddie Condon and Lennie Tristano in 1948.

Of the feature films mentioned above, many, let's say most, were routine programmers,

Harry James co-starred with former band singers Perry Como and Vivian Blaine in *If I'm Lucky* (20th Century Fox, 1946). (*20th Century Fox*)

forgettable in the extreme, and what I remember most from the war years are the luxurious MGM musicals which nearly always featured the bands of Tommy Dorsey and/or Xavier Cugat and/or Harry James. I recall the names of the films, but so unvarying was the formula of sheer escapism that it's hard to separate them in the memory, especially since the stars always seemed to be Esther Williams, Van Johnson, June Allyson, Gloria De Haven and Jimmy Durante. One that does stick in the mind is *Ship Ahoy*, a mid-ocean romp with Eleanor Powell, Red Skelton, Bert Lahr and the Tommy Dorsey orchestra. Probably not one of MGM's greatest musicals, but when I saw it in 1942 I was impressed by an anonymous boy singer with Dorsey, who looked too shy to walk on the set but who sang like a dream. It was a year or so later before the words 'with vocal refrain' disappeared from Dorsey record labels and the scared kid got his first label credits as 'voc. Frank Sinatra'. Dorsey, James and Cugat were inevitable choices for such concentrated screen exposure. Xavier Cugat particularly—with his colourfully costumed orchestra, singers and dancers, the volatile personality of Lina Romay, and the luscious, gay Latin rhythms (not forgetting Cugie's gimmick of holding a chihuahua while conducting!)—was a natural showman, and was often written into the scripts with emphasis on his fractured English and malapropisms. Most bandleaders were given a few dull speaking lines, but Harry James developed as more of a ham than most, and in 20th Century Fox's *Do You Love Me?* he had a leading acting part opposite his old band vocalist Dick Haymes, then at his peak as a musical star. The James and Dorsey bands were not only first-rate musical outfits but looked good, and producers like Arthur Freed and Joe Pasternak had the vision to make good use of such big names once they had them. Dorsey's appearances in *Thousands Cheer, Dubarry Was A*

Benny Goodman and his orchestra share the spotlight with Lynn Bari (who couldn't sing a note but was often cast as a band singer—such was Hollywood!) in *Sweet And Lowdown* (Fox 1944), one of the few musicals built around big band life. (*20th Century Fox*)

Lady, Girl Crazy, Thrill Of A Romance, Broadway Rhythm and *Presenting Lily Mars,* and the fine presentation of the James band in such vehicles as *Two Girls and A Sailor, Bathing Beauty, Springtime In The Rockies, If I'm Lucky, Best Foot Forward* did much to bring modern swing to a wider audience and must certainly have helped make them two of the most popular bandleaders of the forties.

Benny Goodman and his orchestra appeared only peripherally in *Stage Door Canteen* along with many others, but Fox's *Sweet And Lowdown,* although not ranking too highly in Hollywood memorabilia, was nevertheless interesting in that the film was centred round the band and its musicians. But this came a year or two after two definitive films of dance band life, or at least Hollywood's conception of it—there never was a film about musicians unmarred by Hollywood story conventions and stereotyped characters. *Sun Valley Serenade* and *Orchestra Wives* both had their share of screen clichés but they did present Glenn Miller and his orchestra and singers as real people, Miller spoke his lines with more conviction than most, the band was presented intelligently on screen with fine camera work, superb sound (the soundtrack albums are constantly reissued and even today the recorded sound is far ahead of any of that on the Miller studio recordings) and a minimum of dialogue interruptions in the musical numbers.

Ray Eberle, Marion Hutton and the Modernaires sing 'People LikeYou And Me' in *Orchestra Wives.* The famous Glenn Miller saxophone section is (l to r) Tex Beneke, Ernie Caceres, Skip Martin, Al Klink and Willie Schwartz; Maurice Purtill is on drums, Bobby Hackett plays guitar, Miller leads on trombone, and actors Jackie Gleason and Cesar Romero almost look like real musicians on bass and piano. (*20th Century Fox*)

Other leaders, famed on radio for some specific angle to their programmes, took their gimmicks into films. During the thirties Ben Bernie, 'the old maestro', had built up a following by conducting a running 'feud' with columnist-broadcaster Walter Winchell along the lines of the Jack Benny-Fred Allen, Bob Hope-Bing Crosby feuds. A good and successful publicity stunt, Bernie and Winchell did it all over again in two 1937 Fox films, *Love And Hisses* and *Wake Up And Live.* A couple of years later two other popular radio band shows were immortalised on film, as *Pot Of Gold* added a fictional romance between James Stewart and Paulette Goddard to the real life routines of the show of that name starring Horace Heidt and his Musical Knights, and RKO built a series of amusing films around Kay Kyser and his Kollege of Musical Knowledge. Shall we say that I remember them as being amusing in 1939? Times and people change, and the movies have never even surfaced on British television, so one can't be too sure! Kay Kyser wasn't a well-known name in Britain, either then or later, and his radio show was unknown and his records very few, but *That's Right, You're Wrong* and *You'll Find Out, Playmates* and a few later films established Kyser and his singers Ginny Simms, Ish Kabibble, Harry Babbitt and Sully Mason as amiable personalities who could act well in comedy situations, even if the band wasn't very much musically.

Maybe *Some Like It Hot* doesn't really belong in this book, but as far as I'm concerned it deserves plaudits anywhere as the most unbelievable and hilarious story set in dance band surroundings, with Jack Lemmon and Tony Curtis as musicians on the run hiding out, in drag, as members of Sweet Sue And Her Society Syncopators, an all-girls band. The film scored musically as well as visually, with the band and jazz sequences handled on the soundtrack by ex-Paul Whiteman arranger Matty Malneck, who had himself led a successful band in the thirties.

The film world's idea of jazz musicians was customarily as far off the mark as its portrayal of dance bands, the publicly accepted legends about jazzmen and their way of life offering scope for even bigger and better clichés. It has always been denied that Dorothy Baker's novel *Young Man With A Horn* was the story of tragic genius Bix Beiderbecke, but if Miss Baker had even remotely intended it that way the 1950 Warner Brothers film took it right out of the realms of possibility. The tall, handsome, all-American boy hero (Kirk Douglas as Bix?) played pretty commercial songs with the trumpet sound of Harry James at his sweetest, and ended up fit and well playing smoochy obbligatos behind Doris Day's decidedly non-jazz singing. Paramount's *Birth Of The Blues* in 1941 used that old, old bit about the square musician who heard a new kind of music down on the levee and wanted to play it for the people, but with Jack Teagarden and jazz afficionado Bing Crosby on hand,

Everybody's favourite all-girls band! Sweet Sue and her Society Syncopators play 'Runnin' Wild' in *Some Like It Hot*. So what if it wasn't a real band—how many other dance band books give you Marilyn Monroe? (*United Artists*)

as well as some good jazzmen on the soundtrack, it didn't turn out too badly by Hollywood standards. *Blues In The Night*, *Syncopation* and *New Orleans* were notable only for occasional fragments of good music apparent through the typical screen corn. But while two all-coloured films, *Stormy Weather* and *Cabin In The Sky* seem quite condescending in these enlightened days—almost 'Uncle Tom' in their approach to black music and people— the opportunity to see again such legendary performers as Fats Waller, Bill 'Bojangles' Robinson, Cab Calloway and his band and the Nicholas Brothers in the one, and Ethel Waters and Duke Ellington and his orchestra in the other (with Lena Horne in both), is one that can't be missed any time the films come round on television. *Paris Blues* came along in 1961 when movie-makers were more enlightened about many things, and despite the fictional limitations was one of the better films about jazz musicians, with a bonus in a Duke Ellington score and the physical presence of Louis Armstrong. But arguably the best jazz film was *Pete Kelly's Blues*, put together in 1955 by jazz-minded actor-director-producer Jack Webb, who kept obvious commerciality to a minimum. He used the two best girl singers, Ella Fitzgerald and Peggy Lee (who gained an Academy Award for her acting) and authentic jazzmen like Teddy Buckner and the Tuxedo Band, while the music for his 'Big 7' on screen was soundtracked by Matty Matlock's Dixielanders.

Few indeed were the men of the big bands considered worthy of screen biographic

The rehearsal scene in *The Glenn Miller Story* (Universal-International 1954) in which James Stewart, as Miller, allegedly discovered his 'new sound'. It wasn't true, but dramatic enough in context. (*Universal-International*)

honours, though in view of the embellishments, exaggerations and downright inaccuracies contained in any biopic from Madame Curie to Cole Porter this may not have been a bad thing for those omitted from the 'honours list'. But at least Jimmy and Tommy Dorsey, Glenn Miller, Eddy Duchin, Red Nichols and Gene Krupa had enough real-life drama in their careers to warrant 'the treatment'. Anything that may have been lacking in the way of convenient dramatic situations was remedied by the script-writers and, allowing for this, it must be admitted that most of the films were at least good enough on a musical level. *The Fabulous Dorseys* was unique in that Jimmy and Tommy Dorsey starred as themselves, making this otherwise unexceptional film a valuable documentary in big band music. They proved competent enough actors to carry the story line, and with guest spots by their own bands plus recreations of the Scranton Sirens and the early Dorsey Brothers band, and brief appearances of Charlie Barnet, Ziggy Elman, Ray Bauduc, Henry Busse and Art Tatum, the musical side was satisfactory. This despite moments of frustration like the cut from Tatum's solo after four bars to boy-girl dialogue, and the musical inadequacy of a monstrous 'Dorsey Concerto' which brought the brothers together in reconciliation after their father's death. Paul Whiteman conducted as if he didn't believe it either.

In the mid-fifties Universal-International made, and did an excellent job of, *The Glenn Miller Story* and *The Benny Goodman Story*, probably the most satisfactory of all the

Steve Allen goes through the motions while B.G. himself provides the soundtrack music in this scene from Universal-International's *The Benny Goodman Story*. (*Universal-International*)

Danny Kaye, Barbara Bel
Geddes and Harry Guardino in
the 'Follow The Leader'
sequence from *The Five Pennies*,
Paramount's 1959 biopic of
Red Nichols (Kaye). (*Paramount
Pictures*)

movies devoted to big band music, with the exception of Miller's own films. James Stewart
played Miller, his trombone 'playing' coached and dubbed by Joe Yukl, while Steve Allen
as Goodman had B.G.'s own soundtrack assistance. In both cases the music was played by
ex-musicians of the actual bands, and though U-I's music head Joseph Gershenson was
credited with music supervision, it was actually Henry Mancini who was responsible for
the musical accuracy of both films. The Miller story had one fine jam session sequence
with Gene Krupa and the Louis Armstrong All Stars, the other featuring such ex-Good-
manites as Harry James, Lionel Hampton, Teddy Wilson, Ziggy Elman, Krupa and
Martha Tilton. Ben Pollack, an early employer of Miller and Goodman, appeared as
himself in both stories. Forget the fictional gloss, the stereotyped situations and dialogue,
concentrate on the superbly recreated music, and these films will always stand the test of
time. *The Eddy Duchin Story* had Carmen Cavallaro dubbing far better piano than Duchin
ever played, while Tyrone Power portrayed the society leader whose early death from
leukaemia was tastefully handled, being hinted at rather than shown directly. *The Five
Pennies* was Paramount's 1959 tribute to Red Nichols, greatly criticised by the jazz faction
for the choice of Danny Kaye to play Nichols, who dubbed his own playing and even
appeared anonymously in one scene. Louis Armstrong provided most of the musical
highlights while Bob Crosby, Ray Anthony and Bobby Troup were cast as other musicians

Jayne Mansfield was an
improbable but decorative
vocalist with Ray Anthony and
his orchestra in 20th Century
Fox's 1957 rock musical *The
Girl Can't Help It*. (*20th
Century Fox*)

than themselves—typical of front office thinking was the casting of trumpeter Anthony as saxist Jimmy Dorsey. Of *The Gene Krupa Story* (*Drum Crazy* in the UK) I can say nothing, not having seen it. In *Jazz In The Movies* David Meeker says of it that only guest appearances by Red Nichols, Bobby Troup, Anita O'Day and Shelley Manne 'give a few twitches of life to this very stale rags-to-riches show business melodrama', while Stephen Scheuer's *Movies On TV* opines that in this 'corny, highly fictionalised account of Krupa's rise to fame . . . the casting of Sal Mineo as Krupa is another stroke of idiocy'.

This apparent disaster was the last attempt to put big bands on the screen, although in 1969 *They Shoot Horses Don't They?* was set wholly in a dance hall during the thirties marathon dance craze. With a faceless band on the stand throughout, it was a fine opportunity for musical director Johnny Green to recall his own days as a dance band leader in just that period, and the soundtrack resounded to cleverly reconstructed arrangements in the style of the era, including many of Green's own standard songs.

If it seems that there has been an undue emphasis on Hollywood and its product in this chapter, you could just be right. Britain's film industry has never gone in for musicals, and in any case its prewar output was generally unimaginative to the point of tedium. Here again, any shots of dance bands were inevitably in night club sequences, or odd guest spots in corny variety films which were no more than familiar stage acts doing their bit before the camera. The only exceptions were a few feature movies built around the bands of Jack Payne (*Say It With Music*), Jack Hylton (*She Shall Have Music*), Henry Hall (*Music Hath Charms*), Ambrose (*Soft Lights And Sweet Music*) and Harry Roy (*Everything Is Rhythm* and *Rhythm Racketeer*). Other leaders may have had spasmodic engagements as performers, composers or musical directors of prewar British films (Ray Noble wrote the score for the Jack Payne film), but Lew Stone, in addition to arranging for Ambrose and Jack Payne, playing with Roy Fox and finally leading his own band, was also head of music for British and Dominion Films from 1931–3 and for British National in the late thirties, working on and often playing in more than forty films. In postwar years the Ted Heath orchestra found its way into a few features which rarely merited more than B status as well as a few shorts. This, apart from spots by jazz bands of the Acker Bilk-Chris Barber-Kenny Ball type in juvenile 'musicals' of the trad and pop era, is the sad history of British bands on the screen. The fault can hardly be laid at the door of the leaders themselves, rather on a lack of know-how and imagination on the part of film-makers who, unlike their Hollywood counterparts, had either no conception of the importance and popularity of dance and swing bands or of how to present them to advantage.

🎱 THE GRADUATES

Not the least important aspect of the big band scene has been its enduring influence on the entertainment industry via the hundreds of dance band alumni whose experience on the road, on records and in films provided the professionalism and skill that enabled them to build successful careers outside the band business. Obvious examples are of course the great popular singers whose activities as band vocalists have been chronicled in previous chapters—the Crosbys, Sinatras, Fitzgeralds, Lees, Comos and Tormés—but it might prove enlightening to learn just how comprehensive is the list of present day singers, actors, composers and conductors who owe their eminence in varying degrees to their dance band training.

Until the mid-thirties dance band singers sheltered coyly behind the 'With Vocal Refrain' legend on record labels, and the truth is that few of them merited any greater distinction. Crooners were necessary evils as far as musicians were concerned, their sole function being to sing thirty-two bars sandwiched between band choruses in arrangements designed specifically for dancing. In the early days these vocals were all too often handled by either legitimate and strictly non-swinging tenors or any instrumentalist who could remember the words. Sometimes this worked but more often the results were completely forgettable. It was Paul Whiteman, the astute showman, who first realised the importance of spotlighting singers, while the Fred Waring Pennsylvanians were, of course, an almost completely vocal aggregation. But constant exposure with a name band did not necessarily result in instant stardom, and there were many who began and ended their careers as band vocalists, whether through lack of an individual enough talent, lack of opportunity or, in some cases, an absence of the driving ambition essential to survival in an over-crowded profession. Many are the singers whose names, whatever they may have done since, are inextricably linked with the bands with whom they were first associated. Like Bob Eberly and Helen O'Connell, mention of whom inevitably brings to mind the Jimmy Dorsey orchestra of the early forties. For them their days in the limelight ended with their tenure with the band; similarly Ray Eberle and Marion Hutton were such an integral part of the Glenn Miller band that any subsequent work they may have done, Ray in cabaret and Marion in films, is overshadowed by our memories of the Miller years. There are many others, forgotten for thirty years or more, who had their moment of glory singing in front of big bands: Tommy Dorsey's Edythe Wright and Jack Leonard, the thirties vocalists who were forgotten in the acclaim lavished on their successors Frank Sinatra and Jo

The First Lady of Jazz, **Ella Fitzgerald.** (*Polydor Records*)

Girl singers didn't always match looks with talent, but who would argue either aspect of **Fran Warren** (*centre above*) (with Claude Thornhill), **June Christy** (*above*) (Stan Kenton), **Kitty Kallen** (*left below*) (Jack Teagarden, Harry James and Jimmy Dorsey), **Kay Starr** (*left above*) (Glenn Miller, Joe Venuti, Charlie Barnet) or **Eydie Gorme** (*centre below*) (Tex Beneke and Tommy Tucker)? (*MGM Records; Jazz Monthly; Audio Record Review; EMI Records*)

Stafford; Benny Goodman's Martha Tilton, Helen Ward and Louise Tobin; and Orrin Tucker's Bonnie Baker, whose 'Oh Johnny' million-seller failed to open any doors for her as a soloist.

Just as Duke Ellington's musicians seldom achieved the same heights away from the band, so did his singers lack any identity when they left. Ivie Anderson, Joya Sherrill, Kay Davis—it's as Duke's singers rather than successful soloists that they are remembered. The men were rather luckier: Al Hibbler with solo record hits in the fifties and Herb Jeffries as an actor still seen occasionally in TV movies. One of the main faults jazz fans found with the Jimmie Lunceford band was the singing of Dan Grissom, whose sugary style couldn't have been more of an anachronism in the context of that jumping band. Count Basie was more fortunate; in addition to the completely jazz-based singing of Helen Humes and, on occasion, Billie Holiday, the Basie orchestra was graced by the enormous presence of blues singer Jimmy Rushing who had followed through from Walter Page's Blue Devils and the Benny Moten band. His wholly authentic singing was exactly right for the original Basie crew, and when the band itself became just that much more polished in the fifties it was the more sophisticated blues style of Joe Williams that proved a big selling point, both in person and on a hit record of 'Ev'ry Day'.

Among the girl singers, Kitty Kallen brought a fresh young talent to the bands of Jack Teagarden, Harry James and Jimmy Dorsey, a talent which had to be bastardised to conform with the standards of pop stardom in the fifties when her 'Little Things Mean A Lot' became a million seller. A degree of solo success attended the efforts of Claude Thornhill's Fran Warren, who later went on to sing with Art Mooney and his Orchestra and become a fairly successful solo recording artist; Don Cornell, who left Sammy Kaye and had a 1954 hit with 'Hold My Hand', and Helen Forrest, probably the best of all female band singers of the Swing Era. Miss Forrest never put a note wrong on dozens of Harry James and Benny Goodman records, helped them revive their hits years later in hi-fi remakes, and proved that she could still sing with the best of them with Sam Donahue's Tommy Dorsey ghost band of the sixties.

Few British band singers of the thirties were good enough to extend their professional careers beyond the confines of the bandstand for, as I have already noted in Chapter 2, the standard of vocalising in British (and for that matter in American) bands was, with one or two notable exceptions, at best inadequate, at worst quite appalling, and it is hardly surprising that names like Jack Plant, George Barclay, Chips Chippendall and Val Rosing are long forgotten by all but the hard core of thirties enthusiasts. Al Bowlly stands head and shoulders above the rest, an individual and musicianly performer who only once, and without much success, went solo with his own Radio City Rhythm Makers (1937). Otherwise he limited his work to freelance recording sessions with numerous bands and ad hoc orchestras, to supplement his income as resident singer with the bands of Roy Fox and Lew Stone. It must be remembered that as sidemen, which is how they were regarded, vocalists were on a non-royalty basis and in those days session fees were in the nature of £2 to £3 ($5.00 to $7.50) for anything up to eight disc sides. It's highly unlikely that Al Bowlly made a fortune out of his thousand-odd recordings, and equally improbable that any of the singers benefit from LP reissues of their old recordings. The typically British predilection for labelling performers resulted, as already related, in Denny Dennis being billed as 'The British Bing Crosby' and a similar fate awaited Johnny Green, one of Geraldo's wartime team of singers who was more topically billed as 'The British Frank Sinatra'. Since neither Dennis nor Green has been heard of for twenty years or more this was clearly a shortsighted policy, for, comparisons apart, they really were two of the better British singers.

Sharing the Geraldo vocals were Len Camber (male ballads), Dorothy Carless (female ballads), Doreen Villiers (peppy 'hot' singer) and West Indian Archie Lewis who guested with Crosby-type songs. The male-female-peppy blonde set-up was pretty standard fare since the Ambrose days when the roles were filled by Sam Browne, Elsie Carlisle and Evelyn Dall. There was a slight switch in the formula in the postwar Ted Heath Orchestra with ballads by Dickie Valentine and Lita Roza while Dennis Lotis gave the jazzier novelties a male approach. All three made more of their subsequent careers than any of the prewar singers, Valentine in particular having a first-class voice, a gift for impressions, and a sense of humour that made him a vitally talented entertainer, whose death in a car crash robbed the British showbiz scene of one of its best performers. Of the prewar singers only Vera Lynn made it into the bigtime and even now, forty years after her debut with Charlie Kunz and his Casani Club Orchestra followed by her greatest success with Ambrose, she is still very much in demand and singing better than ever with a maturity and musicianship not in evidence during her spell as the World War II 'Forces' Sweetheart'. Others have made their mark in different ways. Sam Costa, pianist-crooner with the Maurice Winnick band was, along with Jack Jackson, one of the earliest British disc jockeys in the fifties; Henry Hall's singer-drummer George Elrick after a spell as bandleader and disc jockey is now in artists' management; Bruce Trent, who joined Jack Hylton as a bass player became a first-class baritone singer who made his name in West End musical comedy; and Alan Kane, one of the busiest and best singers of the thirties and forties, both as freelance and resident with Lew Stone and Ambrose, turned bandleader himself after leaving Mantovani in 1949, and as a drummer has led bands at select West End locations ever since. One of the few musicians from the Golden Age still very active, Alan is now in his seventeenth year at the Wellington Club, London. Other names from the thirties come back through the mists of time—the three sisters Judy Shirley, Shirley Lenner and Anne Lenner, Marjorie Stedeford, Kitty Masters, Pat Hyde, Phyllis Robbins, The Carlyle Cousins, The Rhythm Sisters—all highly rated at the time but strictly of their period.

There was a tremendous improvement in the standard of British band singing after the war. Not only were singers now more important to band presentation, they had emerged during a period when the Sinatras and Fitzgeralds had shown that even a dance band singer working within the limitations of strict tempi could interpret a lyric, and one perfunctory vocal refrain just wasn't enough. Anne Shelton, for whom a spot with the Ambrose orchestra was a stepping stone to higher things, was a 'quality' singer of world class, but has since been limited by the lack of scope in Britain for a richly toned, musicianly singer. Alan Dean, one of the best vocalists in the immediate postwar period, had the same problem but found a market for his talent in America. Paul Carpenter came to Britain with Captain Robert Farnon's Canadian Band Of The AEF and after discharge joined Ted Heath and his Music as compère-singer, Sinatra-influenced with a tendency to sing flat, but became better known as an actor in British films. Geraldo had a strong vocal team after the war with Carole Carr (sister of Dorothy Carless), Sally Douglas and Dick James, who developed into one of the country's finest singers (and, very much later, owner of his own DJM record company, financed by the fortune he accumulated as publisher of Beatle songs). One guest singer with the Geraldo Concert Orchestra was Lee Lawrence, who had sung with Ronnie Pleydell and later became a recording and stage star in his own right, a promising career ended by a tragically early death. Eve Boswell also sang with Geraldo prior to her recording and TV career in the fifties, and Benny Lee, a Scot with a sense of rhythm and a sense of humour, looked like being a potentially good jazz singer during the war years when he recorded with Harry Parry's Radio Rhythm Club Sextet and other bands, but wound up rather more securely as a comedy actor and radio MC. The postwar pattern varied little from that of the thirties and, apart from those specifically mentioned, few British artists outlived their heyday as band singers, the most notable exception being Cleo Laine. Hailed in some quarters as one of the world's great jazz singers Miss Laine is now probably more active as a concert performer than at any time in her twenty-five year career.

Although many name band singers progressed to acting, screen musicals and television specials, some in a genre far removed from their musical origins, there were many who achieved the pinnacle of fame purely as singers, without diversifying into other media. Generally regarded as two of the finest of all jazz singers, Mildred Bailey and Billie Holiday gained valuable experience with bands, although Lady Day's stints with Artie Shaw and Count Basie were interludes rather than the norm. She did her best work, for this listener at least, with the Teddy Wilson Orchestra on the 1935 Brunswicks and with Eddie Heywood's little band on the 1944 Commodores. Mildred Bailey was introduced into the Paul Whiteman orchestra in 1929 by her brother Al Rinker who was one of Whiteman's Rhythm Boys, and also sang with Ben Bernie before teaming up with her then husband Red Norvo in the mid-thirties. Her vocals with Norvo, and with the same orchestra under her own name, represent some of her finest work, and she was well served on many sessions by the scoring of Eddie Sauter and Alec Wilder. Lee Wiley, one of the most subtle and tasteful of jazz-influenced 'torch' singers, is best known for her work with Eddie Condon and his confrères, but she also started out with Whiteman and recorded with Leo Reisman in the early thirties. The later generation of jazz singers is personified by Sarah Vaughan, jazz-taught in the bands of Earl Hines and Billy Eckstine and the Gillespie-Parker small groups, and Dinah Washington. With Sarah, the most powerful influence on contemporary blues

The standard of British band singers improved greatly by the late forties and early fifties, as did their opportunities for solo stardom. Four girls who made it: (r to l) **Carole Carr** and **Eve Boswell** (with Geraldo), **Rose Brennan** (Joe Loss) and the now internationally acclaimed **Cleo Laine,** who sang then, as now, with husband Johnny Dankworth. (*EMI Records, Kenneth Pitt*)

and soul singers, Dinah's first engagement was with the 1944 Lionel Hampton band at the age of twenty. Anita O'Day—that abrasive, hard-driving singer who founded a school of which the most apt pupils were June Christy and Chris Connor who followed her into the Stan Kenton band—first came to prominence with Gene Krupa in 1941–2. Although Lena Horne has for years been one of the world's most potent in-person performers and a vital song-seller, she began in 1935 as an eighteen year old vocalist with Noble Sissle and his Orchestra. Even after making one very minor and unheard-of film and appearing at the Cotton Club, she returned to band singing with Charlie Barnet in 1941, the same year she appeared and recorded with Teddy Wilson at Café Society Downtown. Miss Horne retained her links with the world of big bands when she married Lennie Hayton, a former pianist-arranger with Paul Whiteman. In addition to conducting the MGM Studio

Two distinguished alumni of the swinging years meet a big band buff. **Lena Horne** (ex-Sissle, Barnet and Wilson) and **Lennie Hayton** (former Whiteman pianist-arranger) with the author at the London Palladium in 1952. (*Gramophone Record*)

Rosemary Clooney, originally one of the
Clooney Sisters with Tony Pastor.

Although never a regular band singer,
Dinah Shore featured on records with
such contrasting units as Xavier Cugat and
NBC's Chamber Music Society of Lower
Basin Street. (*EMI Records*)

Orchestra in some of Hollywood's greatest musicals, Hayton also acted as his wife's musical
director until his death. Lena and Lennie, a charming and unassuming couple, made my
very first magazine interview in 1952 a delightfully informal introduction to journalism.

Rosemary Clooney was another warm and human interviewee, happy to talk about the
days of the Tony Pastor band when she and her sister Betty were featured as the Clooney
Sisters. But Kay Starr, while satisfied with her work as Charlie Barnet's vocalist in 1944,
laughed off as a youthful indiscretion the two sides she made with Glenn Miller in 1938 at
the age of sixteen, prior to her early forties work with Joe Venuti and Bob Crosby. The two
finest ballad singers of the forties and stars of many a wartime musical were Dinah Shore
and Ginny Simms. Dinah, although never a regular band singer, had worked with Peter
Dean, Ben Bernie and Xavier Cugat and on NBC's Chamber Music Society of Lower
Basin Street, while Ginny had started singing (incredibly, over forty-five years ago) with
Tom Gerun's band before beginning her long association with Kay Kyser. The technical
expertise which made Jo Stafford one of the great solo performers of the forties and fifties
was already well in evidence in her distinctive vibrato-less lead in the Pied Pipers vocal
group with Tommy Dorsey, and when she graduated to solo work, sharing the stand with
Frank Sinatra and petite Connie Haines (again the format of two ballad singers and a
'personality' swinger) this formidable team gave Dorsey the strongest vocal line-up of any
of the big bands. Jo Stafford married Dorsey arranger Paul Wettstein, who as Paul Weston
became not only her musical director but also a prominent conductor in his own right whose
smooth, richly melodic recordings of evergreens scored for brass, saxes and strings were
the precursors of the 'Mood Music Album' of the early LP era. For me Eydie Gormé was
not only the outstanding voice of the fifties and sixties but also one of the truly great girl
singers of all time; even at this late stage in the game it was still possible for a solo artist to
break into the business via dance bands, in Eydie's case those of Tommy Tucker and Tex
Beneke.

One of the band vocalists who made it into
films in the forties, **Dick Haymes** is
shown here singing with the Harry James
orchestra in 1941. (*Roger Dooner*)

One of the great imperishables, **Perry Como,** who paid his dues back in the thirties with the Ted Weems band. (*EMI Records*)

The genealogy of the male singers has been fairly well charted elsewhere with emphasis on the more obvious name band graduates, but I'm not sure that Dick Haymes wasn't one of the greatest of all, combining Crosby's warmth and tonal richness with Sinatra's sensitivity. His career foundered along the way, but at the time of writing his comeback proves that as a ballad singer he is now supreme. He learned the art while singing with more bands (however temporarily) than almost any other singer, and although his service with Harry James, Tommy Dorsey and Benny Goodman has been fairly well documented, Dick Haymes's earlier experience with the bands of Freddie Martin and Orrin Tucker may be less familiar. His younger brother Bob (who resembled him facially and vocally) became Robert Stanton when he left Carl Hoff's band to try and follow Dick into films, but after some B musicals for Columbia he gave up singing and reverted to being Bob Haymes, songwriter. Andy Russell, one of America's swoon crooners of the mid-forties but who never meant anything in Britain, began as a drummer with Alvino Rey, and Eddie Howard, about the same time, was given the impetus to form his own band after a long spell as singer with Dick Jurgens's orchestra. Four great stars came to the top in the fifties as rugged individualists, film stars, actors and top record sellers, and are so strongly identified with these roles that it is not generally realised that all four were ex-band singers. Possibly this is because none of them ever achieved any eminence in that field, but it is highly probable that singing with dance bands helped them to formulate the styles that eventually did make their names. Dean Martin, for instance, sang with Sam Watkins's band in Cleveland many years before he met up with Jerry Lewis; Gordon Macrae was one of Horace Heidt's battery of singers in the early forties; Guy Mitchell was heard under his real name of Al Cernick on Carmen Cavallaro records circa 1948, and Frankie Laine (after partnering Anita O'Day in marathon dance contests in the early thirties long before either of them dreamed of becoming top singers) replaced Perry Como in Freddie Carlone's band when Como left to join Ted Weems.

In the days when Hollywood musicals were populated by real singers rather than non-singing actors, once more it was the big bands who provided the raw material moulded by the big studios into musical stars. Morton Downey, the tenor who starred in early talkies and the night club circuit, had actually been the very first dance band singer *per se* when he joined Paul Whiteman in the early twenties. As vocals were normally handled by instrumentalists, he sat in the band holding a saxophone so that this departure from the norm would not appear too radical. Downey later sang with Jan Garber's band and on radio with Raymond Paige and his Orchestra. Alice Faye, the best-loved of all 20th Century Fox's blonde stars, was singing with the Rudy Vallee orchestra when Vallee brought her to Hollywood to appear opposite him in *George White's Scandals Of 1934*. After Miss Faye married bandleader Phil Harris and lost interest in acting she was succeeded at Fox by

Dance band singing was good groundwork for the subsequent musical careers of **Betty Hutton** (*above left*) (with Vincent Lopez), **Jane Russell** (*right*) (Kay Kyser), (*l to r*) **Tony Martin** (Tom Gerun, Ray Noble etc), **Guy Mitchell** (he was Al Cernick on Carmen Cavallaro records), and **Gordon Macrae** (Horace Heidt). (*Paramount Pictures; 20th Century Fox; Gramophone Record Review; Warner Bros. Films*)

ex-Ted Fio Rito vocalist Betty Grable and another former band singer, Vivian Blaine. Two of the principal musical leads at Paramount Pictures were Dorothy Lamour, who had begun her career in the mid-thirties as crooner with the band of her husband Herbie Kay, and Betty Hutton, whose uninhibited vocal antics had enlivened the appearances of Vincent Lopez and his Orchestra.

Mention has been made elsewhere of the name band careers of Gloria De Haven (with Bob Crosby and Jan Savitt), Janet Blair (Hal Kemp) and Marilyn Maxwell (Ted Weems), but the classic example of a band singer who became a world star is, of course, Doris Day. As sixteen year old Doris Kappelhoff she had her first professional engagements with Barney Rapp and his New Englanders (who actually worked out of Cleveland, Ohio) prior to fulfilling odd dates with Fred Waring and his Pennsylvanians and the Bob Crosby band before beginning her long and ultimately successful stint with Les Brown and his Band Of Renown. Fred Waring, whose Lane Sisters vocal act eventually resolved itself into three separate and equally talented actresses, Rosemary, Priscilla and Lola, also brought choral director Kay Thompson into the limelight, or such part of it as was allowed to shine on a 'back room girl' whose activity as vocal coach and arranger on MGM musicals of the forties was finally to be superseded when Miss Thompson became herself a successful night club entertainer and authoress. Essentially Broadway and cabaret artists, both Pearl Bailey and

Doris Day took a 'Sentimental Journey' with Les Brown's Band of Renown that led to the top of her profession. (*Warner Bros. Films*)

Ella Logan also appeared in films; Pearl, a jazz-based singer of 'point' songs, learned her jazz (and possibly her marvellous timing) as singer with Cootie Williams and his mid-forties band, and Ella was a Scots lass who worked with Jack Hylton before finding stardom in America in films like *52nd Street* and on Broadway in *Finian's Rainbow*. Saxophonist Al Norris sang occasionally while playing with the bands of Tom Gerun and Anson Weeks before receiving greater recognition as Tony Martin; even after he had appeared in films he recorded with Ray Noble and his Orchestra, and during the war was the original vocalist with Major Glenn Miller's Army Air Force Band before going on to more serious duties in the Far East, which earned him a Presidential citation and the Bronze Star. Perhaps one of the more surprising graduates was opera singer James Melton who, en route to the New York Metropolitan, had been a saxophone player in dance bands and a member of the Revellers, a popular singing act of the late twenties and early thirties. Many famous songwriters began as dance band musicians—Harold Arlen, Sammy Cahn and Saul Chaplin among them—but the outstanding example is Johnny Mercer, yet another young hopeful given his start by Paul Whiteman as singer-MC, a role he also filled with Benny Goodman later.

The transition from dance band singer to musical star is perhaps to be expected, given a combination of talent and opportunity, but what may be less obvious is the number of legitimate actors who graduated from dance music. Before he made his screen debut in *All Quiet On The Western Front* Lew Ayres was a banjo player with Henry Halstead and his band, and Dick Powell sang and played trumpet, saxes and banjo with the Royal Peacock Orchestra in Louisville in 1925, joining trumpeter Charlie Davis's Orchestra shortly afterwards. Fred MacMurray was a saxophone player with Gus Arnheim and his Orchestra at the age of nineteen, and was featured as a member of the California Collegians in the original Broadway production of *Roberta*, the break that took him to Hollywood. Comedy actor Art Carney was, in his youth, with the Horace Heidt band as a member of the Donna and Her Don Juans vocal group; veteran actor Leif Ericson sang with Ted Fio Rito around

1933; and a contemporary television favourite, Gene Barry, was heard as vocalist with the Teddy Powell orchestra in the early forties. Jerry Colonna, who enlivened so many Hope-Crosby *Road* films with his cameos, was a CBS studio trombonist who sat in with Jimmy Dorsey's band, and Art Lund, still remembered for his 1946 record of 'Blue Skies' with Benny Goodman, later became a stage star in *The Most Happy Fella* and is now seen in television crime series. Pat O'Malley now plays aged Irishmen, policemen, hoboes, bartenders and assorted venerable characters in whom it is hard to see the erstwhile romantic young balladeer in Jack Hylton's band of forty years ago, and former child star Jackie Cooper, now a TV actor-director, played drums with a Claude Thornhill US Navy Band in the Pacific during the war. Dale Evans, better known as Mrs Roy Rogers, sang with Anson Weeks in San Francisco before getting to share the limelight with Trigger the wonder horse and even Jane Russell took to the road with Kay Kyser between films. It might be stretching the facts somewhat to claim two of the screen's most rugged 'tough guys' as dance band graduates, but in a way it's quite true. Both Paul Douglas and Broderick Crawford were Glenn Miller's radio announcers, Douglas working for CBS on Miller's Chesterfield programmes several years before his acting career began, and a much younger and slimmer Sergeant Broderick Crawford doing similar chores on the staff of the Army Air Force Band both in America and Europe.

With the demise of the band business and the influx of big band arrangers into the recording and film studios, the writers who had helped formulate the many different styles of music heard during the previous decades had a heaven-sent opportunity to explore their own musical paths. I have already touched upon this aspect of postwar music in Chapter 5, emphasising the work of arrangers who continued in swing music and its variations. Many others, however, broadened their own horizons and not being limited by the brass-saxes-and-rhythm formula brought their considerable talents to what had previously been called 'light' music, adding to that pallid product their own experience of rhythmic music and in many cases finding intriguing new voicings for the ever-larger string sections which an increasingly prosperous record industry could now afford to hire for its sessions. Compare the pleasant, but obviously financially restricted backings men like Victor Young and John Scott Trotter provided for Bing Crosby in the thirties with the monumental backgrounds Axel Stordahl created for Frank Sinatra a decade later. With singers such as these, who needed no musical crutch for their supreme vocal talent, it didn't really matter, but it could work wonders for less talented artists.

The renaissance in light music in the mid-thirties, which lifted it straight out of the salon on to the concert platform, figuratively speaking, was due to André Kostelanetz who made some brilliant Brunswick records which haven't been in circulation, in Britain at least, since their original issue on 78s. With arrangements by *inter alia* Claude Thornhill and George Bassman, and top people like Glenn Miller and the Dorseys playing on the sessions, Kostelanetz 'legitimised' jazz numbers like 'Tiger Rag' and Don Redman's 'Chant Of The Weed', and jazzed-up (only in the very broadest sense, I must add) traditional tunes. Although these now sound dated inasmuch as they are very much of their own period in time, the quality and imagination of the scoring and playing show that Kostelanetz and his writers were so advanced as to make everything else happening at the time seem inexpressibly effete. David Rose and Percy Faith also increased the prestige of light music by their emergent work of the forties in which expert musicianship and increasingly sophisticated arrangements gave their orchestras an individual style. Both accented strings but could also swing convincingly, and in fact I have always regarded Faith's brass section as one of the finest ever, inside or outside the big band field as such. Raymond Paige and Mark Warnow were studio conductors whose combination of strings and a normal dance band complement weren't always too righteous but produced excellent ballad effects, if somewhat stiff (all right, if you insist, corny!) on rhythm numbers.

But these were all men whose connection with the big bands was tenuous if it existed at all (though Mark Warnow was Raymond Scott's brother) and it was only in the post-Big Band Era that the graduates began to make their presence felt, following a pattern which Victor Young was one of the earliest conductors to establish. Violinist with Ted Fio Rito and Dan Russo's Oriole Orchestra and the Ben Pollack band, Young became very much an 'in' studio man, conducting hundreds of Decca vocal sessions and just as many film scores for Paramount and other companies. The super-efficiency of his work as songwriter, film composer, arranger and conductor was not always matched by a correspondingly high standard of playing on his orchestral albums, which lacked the depth and style of the Roses and Faiths. Gordon Jenkins explained this to me once by saying, 'Victor always had a bad band. He was a wonderful man, but a pushover for hard luck stories from relatives and out of work musicians, and he used them all on his sessions.' Jenkins himself was safe from any such strictures. A keen pianist who had hung around the Grand Terrace in Chicago with Earl Hines, he was also a warm and sympathetic arranger who had done much for the Isham Jones and Woody Herman bands (and provided Benny Goodman with his signing-off theme, 'Goodbye'). He made some marvellous choral-orchestral records in the forties and provided singers like Frank Sinatra and Nat King Cole with some of the most emotional accompaniments ever heard. Salvatore ('Tutti' or 'Toots') Camarata, now a legitimate conductor, was in his early years a trumpet player and/or arranger with the Casa Loma Orchestra, Jimmy Dorsey, Charlie Barnet and Paul Whiteman; Paul Weston had worked for Bob Crosby and Tommy Dorsey in whose band he shared arranging chores with Axel Stordahl (Axel sang in Dorsey's vocal trio before the arrival of the Pied Pipers); and Warner Brothers recording executive Sonny Burke had led his own band in addition to his work with Jimmy Dorsey, Charlie Spivak and Frank Sinatra. The 1945-6 Woody Herman Herd was full of good writers who all contributed to the library, none more eminent in later years than pianist Ralph Burns who had graduated via Red Norvo and Charlie Barnet and went on to Broadway and Hollywood, and trumpeter Neal Hefti, who also played and wrote for Alvino Rey, Georgie Auld and Count Basie, probably his finest hour jazz-wise, before he also proceeded to uplift the standard of film and television music.

'Music By De Vol' has become a familiar credit in these media, but long before Frank De Vol took up writing for (and sometimes acting in) films, he was a prolific producer of fifties mood music albums and yet another graduate, in his case from playing saxophone and arranging for Horace Heidt and Alvino Rey. Leroy Holmes, orchestral conductor and arranger for United Artists Records, served his time with Harry James and Vincent Lopez, and Skip Martin, who did some fine swinging scores for the MGM Studio Orchestra

Leroy Holmes had his first band in Phoenix in 1934, arranged for Vincent Lopez and Harry James (for whom he wrote 'The Mole', 'Prince Charming' etc) before graduating to the recording studios as arranger-conductor. (*MGM Records*)

on film soundtracks, had his start with Charlie Barnet and Les Brown, working in the latter band with Frank Comstock, who also did a number of albums under his own name. Two of the currently popular names in British light music are Ronnie Aldrich and Tony Osborne; Aldrich's double-tracked piano albums with the London Festival Orchestra are a far cry from his jazz days with the Squadronaires, and although Osborne also features himself on piano I first saw him playing trumpet with the Cyril Stapleton band around 1947. But perhaps the most unusual graduate from the Swing Era is conductor Les Baxter who, although a classically trained pianist, had his only big band experience as a singer, a member of Mel Tormé's Mel-tones with Artie Shaw in 1945. Skitch Henderson had his own band until invited to join Frank Sinatra as musical director, since when he has become a top-ranking radio, television and concert conductor. Harry Gold's Pieces Of Eight, a popular British Dixieland group of the forties, proved a good if somewhat unorthodox

Former trumpeter with Harry Gold's Pieces of Eight, **Ron Goodwin** has brought an individual and recognisable style to film composing. (*EMI Records*)

nursery for embryo conductor-arrangers, producing trombonist Geoff Love, pianist Norrie Paramor (ex-Jack Harris, Sydney Kyte and Maurice Winnick) and trumpeter Ron Goodwin, all of whom are still very active in all branches of light and concert music, Goodwin particularly being one of the film industry's most talented and prolific screen composers.

It's interesting to note how functioning in more exalted circles encourages a certain formality among former dance band musicians—Messrs Green, Dankworth, Scott and Keating were all 'Johnny' in the old days, but have now become much more dignified 'Johns'. Wally Stott, a great swing writer and former alto sax with Geraldo, became Walter Stott when conducting more serious recordings, but the problem of dual identity was resolved in the early seventies when Wally/Walter became Angela Morley, an event without precedent in the band business, and is still very active in making the new name as familiar as the old. During a spell as recording manager at Chappell's I had the great pleasure of working with both Wally and Peter Yorke, an illustrious name in British music and a truly gentle man. Beginning as pianist with Percival Mackey's orchestra in 1927, Yorke recorded with the Rhythm Makers before joining Jack Hylton with whom he made his name as a fine concert arranger. With Louis Levy and his Gaumont British Symphony, Peter Yorke created a weighty but effective style in writing dance tunes for big band and strings that he perpetuated after the war with his own Concert Orchestra featuring the alto of Freddy Gardner—technically brilliant, but by then dated and devoid of the jazz influence that had informed Gardner's session work in the thirties.

I have already paid tribute to Henry Mancini's position as an originator of screen and TV 'crime jazz', but Mancini didn't just suddenly appear from nowhere. As a twenty-year old soldier he tried to join Major Glenn Miller's Army Air Force Band but was turned down. He made it eventually, but only after the band returned to civvy street, and he worked as pianist-arranger for Tex Beneke and the Miller band until 1951 when he joined Universal-International Pictures as a sort of musical oddbody. This meant he did everything from writing, supervising, arranging, conducting, or just plain 'scissors-and-paste' jobs on library music. But he was the ideal man to reconstitute the scores of Glenn Miller and Benny Goodman when the studio filmed their biopics in 1954-5, and it was then but a short step to creating his own kind of swing for *Peter Gunn*. Hollywood also has to thank the big bands for the presence of Johnny Mandel, ex-trombonist with Alvino Rey, Boyd Raeburn, Artie Shaw and others, and fellow-trombonist Nelson Riddle who had graced the bands of Tommy Dorsey, Les Elgart, Bob Crosby and Alvino Rey with his playing and writing presence. As a film writer Riddle follows the best Hollywood traditions, but it is his recording work over the years that stamps him as one of the most versatile and consistent graduates. While his orchestra is always immaculately organised, Riddle's swinging beat comes through in one of the best rhythm sections since Basie. The Riddle orchestra has power and depth, which many bands have lacked, and this, allied to his trademark of sustained strings adding tension to the brass and saxes phrasing (both in his vocal support for Frank Sinatra, Dinah Shore, Ella Fitzgerald etc or in his own solo albums), makes him possibly the finest example of a Swing Era musician and big band graduate who has carried over the best of music from that period into contemporary orchestral music.

9 THE EUROPEAN SCENE

Regarded in the context of big band music as a whole, European contributions must be infinitesimal. Not necessarily negligible as we shall see, but certainly the continent has never been an important breeding ground for jazz or dance music. It's quite a paradox, therefore, that while this book is being written in 1976 the largest record sales ever achieved by big bands are being notched up by two German orchestras and, for what must be the first time in popular music history, American and British bands are copying *them*.

The leading prewar French band was that of Ray Ventura, whose Collegians boasted a larger personnel than the average three brass-three saxes-three rhythm continental band. The French counterpart of Whiteman and Hylton, Ventura had a long and successful career as a bandleader before going into publishing, but if he is known to today's generation it is as the uncle of singing star Sacha Distel. Europe's outstanding contribution to jazz was of course the Quintet Of The Hot Club Of France, in which Stephane Grappelly's lightly swinging violin was superbly complemented by the virtuoso guitar of Django Reinhardt, a one-man rhythm section who scarcely needed the support of the guitars of his brother Joseph and Roger Chaput. Louis Vola on bass was the fifth man, and occasional vocals were provided by Jerry Mengo, who was to become a prominent bandleader himself after the war. When the quintet was separated on the outbreak of war neither Grappelly in London nor Reinhardt in Paris was able to recapture that rapport, though both still made

Stephane Grappelli. (*Polydor Records*)

116

good music by any standards. Django died in 1953 but Grappelly is still highly active and, in his late sixties, is playing better than ever. Members of the quintet often formed the nucleus of big bands accompanying such visiting American jazzmen as Coleman Hawkins, Bill Coleman, Benny Carter, Eddie South, Frank 'Big Boy' Goodie, Dickie Wells and Rex Stewart, and four sides made by Hawkins with Michael Warlop's Orchestra in 1935 are now collectors' items. Featured on these was the trumpet of Arthur Briggs, who had come to Europe in 1929 with the Noble Sissle Orchestra. Another US exile was pianist-arranger Freddie Johnson who settled in France about the same time after visiting Paris with Sam Wooding's orchestra. Together Briggs and Johnson formed a mixed American-European band, Johnson later going to Holland where he organised a nine-piece outfit with Dutch reed player Lex Van Spall. Holland was at this time supporting a number of dance bands, among them Mitchell's Band at the Scheveningen Casino, Melle Weersma's Red White And Blue Aces at the Central Hotel in Den Haag (Weersma came to England in 1935 to join Jack Hylton), Louis De Vries And His Internationals and, probably the best-remembered Dutch band by virtue of their recording association with Coleman Hawkins, Theo Massman's Ramblers Dance Orchestra.

Denmark had Eric Tuxen and his Orchestra at the Copenhagen Arena, Vilfred Kjaer and his Danish Rhythm Club Orchestra, also in Copenhagen at the Valencia, and quartets led by violinists Svend Asmussen and Eli Donde, both based unashamedly on Joe Venuti's Blue Four. In Belgium a kind of hot jazz was played by Charles Remue's New Stompers, and the principal big bands were led by two of the country's foremost trumpeters. Gus De Loof fronted his Radiolians prior to working in Paris with Ray Ventura and as a session musician in French film studios, while Robert De Kers And His Cabaret Kings built up a considerable reputation during their residency at the Century Hotel in Antwerp.

Theo Uden Masman's **Ramblers Dance Orchestra,** the leading Dutch band of the thirties, are pictured here with Coleman Hawkins, with whom they made a set of historic recordings in 1935.

In view of the Nazi attitude to non-Aryan, neo-Fascist, decadent western swing, it is surprising that so many prominent dance bands could be found in prewar Hitler Germany. There was Teddy Stauffer and his Original Teddies, while both Heinz Wehner and James Kok—one of the few continental leaders of the early thirties to feature as many as five brass, five saxes and four rhythm—had big bands that inclined towards the Jimmie Lunceford and Casa Loma repertoire. It may be conjecture, but perhaps the notorious Teutonic precision dictated an approach to dance music calling for mechanical accuracy rather than the rhythmic freedom of the American swing bands. Marek Weber's orchestra achieved a worldwide reputation, but excellent though the orchestra was, Weber is remembered more for Viennese waltzes and light music than for any effective contribution to the world of big bands. Pianist Peter Kreuder had a pleasant combo playing cocktail

Kurt Edelhagen and his Orchestra
reintroduced the big band sound to
postwar Germany. (*Polydor Records*)

lounge music and was still recording, or at least his records were still being issued in
America, in the early sixties. There was also a band of which I have no personal knowledge
but which I believe had a reputation in Germany at one time, called Die Goldene Sieben
(The Golden Seven).

Obviously World War II caused somewhat of a hiatus in European dance music and
jazz, though not a complete cessation. Django Reinhardt continued playing in France,
teaming up with clarinettist Hubert Rostaing, while the Dutch Swing College Band
emerged from the underground movement in Holland during the war. Their musical policy
changed from the Ellington small group style to the revivalist 'trad' jazz of the sixties, and
it is only in recent years that the band has loosened up into a good Dixieland outfit. After
the war there were a host of new American influences to be assimilated, and the influx of
American jazzmen into Europe on an even larger scale than before the war, as well as the
wider distribution of records, made continental musicians vastly more swing and jazz
conscious than they had been, even if the results were often little more than carbon copies
of the transatlantic prototype. The outstanding band of the late forties and early fifties was
that of Kurt Edelhagen who, like Britain's Vic Lewis, appeared dedicated to the works of
Stan Kenton but who later modified his style and recorded some first-class dance music
with strings. Belgian conductor Francis Bay and his Orchestra commemorated their
appearance at the 1958 Brussels Exhibition with a series of recorded 'tributes' to Ellington,
Basie, Harry James and many other swing band leaders, even including Britain's Ted Heath
and Mantovani—'tribute' being a euphemism for 'carbon copy'. Other bands of various
sizes and styles grew up, led by French trumpeter Aime Barelli, Italian altoist Fausto
Papetti, German violin virtuoso Helmut Zacharias and pianist Fritz Schultz-Reichel,
who also gained fame for his honky-tonk piano records under the pseudonym of Crazy
Otto. In the early fifties Sweden was a favoured location for American jazzmen of the

Aimé Barelli. (*Disques Pathe*)

In these seventies it is Germany's **Bert Kaempfert** who keeps big band music not only alive but an extremely viable commercial proposition. (*Polydor Records*)

calibre of Stan Getz, but despite a plethora of small group 'cool' jazz recordings by such talented native musicians as Arne Domnerus, Lars Gullin, Bengt Hallberg *et al*, only a handful of excellent 'progressive' big band sessions directed by Arne Lamberth made much impression.

The North German Radio Dance Orchestra was one of the finest musical aggregations in that country, attracting top playing and arranging talent—Eddie Sauter worked with the band for a time. And among the men drawn to its ranks in 1955 was a twenty-six year old bass player named James Last who had been leading his own Last-Becker Sextet for seven years. Last now started scoring for the orchestra and eventually formed his own band, which he adapts for any style from the neo-symphonic to a Hammond organ combo, but which is now best known for brassy performances of sing-along medleys of pop tunes and standards. Although removed considerably from what we have regarded in this book as big band music, Last nevertheless warrants inclusion as the most commercially successful and widely plagiarised band in popular music at a time when pop and rock had supposedly driven bands of any description clear out of the market place. The other German maestro, responsible for making quality dance music a viable propostion not only in his own country but throughout the world, is multi-instrumentalist-composer-arranger-conductor Bert Kaempfert. Like James Last, Kaempfert is somewhat of a musical chameleon, but the basic Kaempfert style is a rich ensemble sound founded on good, danceable tempi, combining the repertoire of the times with the nostalgic flavour of the Swing Era, yet managing to produce a completely original brand of big band music which not only owes nothing to outside influences but is itself proving an influence on bands elsewhere.

These are not dance bands as such. Last does concert tours and Kaempfert seldom emerges from the recording studios, but their continued success on records does keep big band music, in however bastardised a form, alive just a little longer.

10 THE END? AS IT IS NOW

Is it quite true to say that big bands are dead? Certainly, if one thinks in terms of the thirties and forties when the world was full of dance bands travelling on one night stands, when ballrooms drew capacity business and every big hotel had its resident band. Judged by those standards the prognosis is far from optimistic. But there is still a band business of sorts, its activities mainly transferred to other media. The BBC retains its resident orchestras and allots regular air space to outside bands such as Billy Ternent, Joe Loss, Ken Mackintosh, Jack Dorsey *et al*, but the greatest service to lovers of our kind of music is provided by Alan Dell, whose 'Dance Band Days' and 'Big Band Sound' record programmes are an oasis in a desert of musical trash.

At the time of writing there is a minor boom in the sounds of the forties, even among the younger element of 'pop' fans who, for some undefinable reason, have started jiving in discotheques to Glenn Miller records. In Britain a single television programme by Jack Parnell and his orchestra has sparked off a regular series designed to take viewers down a nostalgic road of Swing Era memories, while many of Parnell's freelance musicians, including other Ted Heath alumni, reformed under trumpeter Stan Reynolds under the somewhat hyperbolic title of The Greatest Swing Band In The World. The New Paul Whiteman Orchestra exists, not in America, as an 'old boys' reunion, as might be expected, but in Britain as a thirty-three piece unit formed by leading London session men, many former bandleaders in their own right, dedicated to the recorded and concert presentation of Whiteman scores of the late twenties. Recalling a similar time and place, the Pasadena Roof Orchestra has taken over the mantle of the Temperance Seven in the idiomatic presentation of songs of the twenties and thirties.

The vogue for pseudo-Miller music mentioned elsewhere was expanded in 1976 to include the neo-symphonic sound of Glenn Miller's Army Air Force Orchestra recreated by the Million Airs, who also put up the House Full notices whenever they appear in concert. Straws in the wind? Ephemeral trends born of keen business management? Who can say? By the time this appears in print it might be all over and the trend bypassed in favour of some other craze, but that it was able to happen at all in a completely alien musical climate is an encouraging sign.

Early in 1975 came the news that veterans Frankie Carle and Freddie Martin had taken new bands on the road throughout the States, and concert audiences on both sides of the Atlantic still welcome the regular visits of such Swing Era hold-outs as Count Basie, Woody Herman, Buddy Rich and Harry James. Until 1974 it seemed as though the ageless Duke Ellington would go on for ever, but with Duke's passing a whole era died. Although the Ellington Orchestra still functions under his son's direction, Mercer Ellington's first positive action was to sack all the familiar faces that had made his father's music so personal. It remains to be seen whether the Ducal spirit can be maintained by a young orchestra none of whose members can have any affinity with his music, or whether this will become just another 'ghost band' going through the motions.

There have been spasmodic attempts to revive big band jazz with (mostly short-lived) new bands comprising a mixture of experienced and tyro musicians, chief among them the Thad Jones-Mel Lewis Orchestra and the Kenny Clarke-Francy Boland Big Band. Here, as a vindication of everything that leaders like Goodman, Barnet and Shaw fought for thirty years before, old barriers came tumbling down with coloured and white musicians, American, British and European, working together with one common interest, speaking

Former trombonist-arranger with many Swing Era bands, **Ray Conniff** revived the big band style in the mid-fifties with his scoring for voices in unison with instrumental sections. (*Audio Record Review*)

the universal language of music. Former Kenton trumpeter Maynard Ferguson, having led an American band with his own spectacular but not always tasteful solo and lead playing, settled in Britain some years ago and built a modern and occasionally rock-influenced band from local musicians, but even his most outrageous effects paled beside the 'unorthodox' orchestra of Don Ellis, whose amplified trumpet was just one of the bizarre effects. Although British ballrooms are generally geared to more mechanical forms of music-making, Bob Miller and the Millermen, Johnny Howard, Ken Mackintosh, Tony Evans, Ray McVay and the perenniel Joe Loss and their bands have all found steady employment over the last few years. For it is one of those paradoxes which make this business so unpredictable that ballroom dancing, with its formal dress, stylised techniques and reliance on 'evergreen' dance music, remains in favour at a time when pop music and discos have freed the younger generation from the routines of conventional dancing. Something like half the time allotted to the International Ballroom Championships is occupied by the Juvenile and Junior Trophies, indicating that more youngsters than we perhaps realise have come to enjoy the discipline of formalised dancing and the sense of occasion inseparable from an evening devoted to this form of escapism.

Yet even without this typically British outlet for dance music one has only to open one's ears to other forms of entertainment to realise that, far from being dead or even moribund, big band music is the very cornerstone of contemporary show business. Less obviously than in the sweet and swinging years certainly, but just think about it for a moment. Take pop records—a goodly percentage, with special emphasis on the Tamla Motown and Memphis 'soul' output, depend largely on big band support, and numerous pop groups inspired by the example of Blood, Sweat and Tears double on brass and saxes to create their own accompaniments. Let's not forget BBC-TV's weekly *Top Of The Pops* which has for years relied on Johnny Pearson's remarkably efficient and versatile big band as a musical crutch for its guest artists. And isn't it surprising that all the station breaks on BBC radio's pop channels are provided by forties-type vocal groups with swing band backings? Television—not only are many commercials recorded by big band musicians, but musical shows are founded on brass and saxes rather than strings, while the various crime and comedy series rely on jazz-influenced scoring by such big band alumni as Johnny Mandel, Quincy Jones, Neal Hefti, Dominic Frontiere, Oliver Nelson *et al* in addition to newcomers who seem to fall readily into the style. Films—well, this is where it all started, and we can pinpoint the beginning with Elmer Bernstein's modern, brassy score for *The Man With The Golden Arm* in 1955. He followed up a few years later with *Walk On The Wild Side*, Duke Ellington wrote entire jazz scores for *Anatomy Of A Murder* (1959), *Paris Blues* (1961), *Assault On A Queen* (1966) and *Change Of Mind* (1969) and Eddie Sauter's score for *Mickey One* (1965) featuring Stan Getz was another milestone.

Fifty years after he started broadcasting from Gleneagles **Henry Hall** returned to the Scottish hotel in 1974 to lead a specially assembled 'reunion' orchestra. (*Henry Hall*)

But in all truth we must regard Henry Mancini's *Peter Gunn* (originally on TV and later on the big screen) as the principal influence, a new aspect of big band jazz used in a different medium that opened doors for Nelson Riddle, Billy May, Michel Legrand, Quincy Jones, Lalo Schifrin and many others. This is a new type of film music, a million light years removed from the Viennese romanticism of the Waxmans, Steiners, Korngolds and Kapers, but wholly in keeping with the faster pace of modern movie-making. The James Bond series with their ferocious John Barry scores were typical of the trend (though it's interesting that the Bond theme itself was written not by Barry but by Monty Norman, a former singer with Stanley Black's dance band).

Far from big bands being dead, it is inescapably obvious that their influence has so permeated the entire entertainment scene over the years that they are, and always will be, one of the basic elements of popular music. I don't for one moment envisage the return of the halcyon years of the dance bands. Popular music, dancing and listening have, for better or for worse, taken on a new dimension. Those of us whose tastes were formulated by the songs of Gershwin, Porter, Arlen and Wilder cannot adapt our standards to accommodate the mini-talents of the contemporary 'singer-songwriters' any more than those weaned on the composing and orchestrating genius of Duke Ellington or Eddie Sauter are likely to be madly thrilled by the banal melodies and harmonies of pop groups whose work is aimed at the lowest common denominator of untutored public taste. Or, even worse, the wail of the dreaded Moog! To all but the most altruistic record companies (and there are some) we are the forgotten generation, dependent upon vintage reissues for our entertainment with only an occasional Bert Kaempfert or Count Basie to leaven the output of new recordings.

But there's always hope, not for a return of the halcyon years but at least that the status quo may be maintained. In a September 1971 edition of *Variety*, Willis Conover, a man who has done so much for jazz and swing on radio for The Voice Of America, spoke of the increasingly young audience for jazz concerts and went on to make this statement:

Today there are some five hundred big bands in universities [and thousands in high schools] playing jazz. I can't believe that when all these youngsters graduate they are not going to continue their interest in playing or listening to good music.

Benny Goodman today. (*Polydor Records*)

Good music is timeless. For me at least the best of swing and dance music is as valid today as it ever was regardless of its period of origin. (It is because of this quality of timelessness, the feeling that the best of dance music is always with us, that I have generally omitted much biographical data on the bandleaders who made it so, especially dates of birth and death; the former are a matter of public record in any reference book, the latter occur with distressing frequency as a reminder that physically the practitioners of music age more than the music itself.)

If this new generation mentioned by Mr Conover maintains the high standards, in whatever media, set by their predecessors, then sanity may yet prevail.

BIBLIOGRAPHY

ALLEN, Stewart. *Stars of Swing* (British Yearbooks Ltd, London 1946)

BARNES, Ken. *Sinatra and the Great Song Stylists* (Ian Allan, Shepperton 1972)

BATON. *Famous British Bandleaders* (Danceland Publications Ltd, London 1947)

CROSBY, Bing. *Call Me Lucky* (Frederick Muller Ltd, London 1955)

DANCE, Stanley. *World of Duke Ellington* (Macmillan Ltd, London 1971)

DELAUNEY, Charles. *New Hot Discography* (Criterion Music Corp, New York 1948)

EDWARDS, Ernie Jnr. *Sound of Claude Thornhill and His Orchestra* (Erngeobil Publications, Whittier, California 1967)

FLOWER, John. *Moonlight Serenade* (Arlington House, New York 1972)

GRAHAM, Vic. *Band Parade* (Roy Croft/Fanfare Publications, London c1947)

KEEPNEWS, Orrin and GRAUER, Bill Jnr. *Pictorial History of Jazz* (Spring Books, London 1960)

LESLIE, Peter. *Big Bands of the Thirties* (New English Library, London 1971)

McCARTHY, Albert. *The Dance Band Era* (Spring Books, London 1974)

——. *Big Band Jazz* (Studio Vista, London 1974)

McCARTHY, Albert and CAREY, Dave. *Jazz Directory* (Cassell & Co Ltd, London 1957)

MEEKER, David. *Jazz in the Movies* (British Film Institute, London 1972)

PANASSIÉ, Hugues and GAUTIER, Madeleine. *Dictionary of Jazz* (Cassell & Co Ltd, London 1956)

PAYNE, Jack. *Signature Tune* (Stanley Paul Ltd, London c1946)

ROWE, John. *Swing Souvenir* (Findon Publications, London c1946)

RUST, Brian. *The Dance Bands* (Ian Allan, Shepperton 1972)

——. *Discography of British Dance Bands* (Storyville Publications, Essex 1974)

SANFORD, Herb. *Tommy and Jimmy—The Dorsey Years* (Arlington House, New York; Ian Allan, Shepperton 1972)

SCHLEMAN, Hilton. *Rhythm on Record* (Melody Maker, London 1936)

SHAW, Artie. *The Trouble with Cinderella* (Farrar, Straus & Young, New York 1952)

SIMON, George T. *The Big Bands* (Macmillan & Co, New York and London 1967)

——. *Simon Says—Sights and Sounds of the Swing Era* (Arlington House, New York 1971)

——. *Glenn Miller and His Orchestra* (W. H. Allen, London 1974)

TAYLOR, John Russell and JACKSON, Arthur. *The Hollywood Musical* (Secker & Warburg, London 1971)

TREADWELL, Bill. *Big Book of Swing* (Cambridge House, New York 1946)

TRODD, Kenith. *Lew Stone—A Career in Music* (Joyce Stone, London 1971)

VEDEY, Julien. *Band Leaders* (Rockliff Publishing Corp Ltd, London 1950)

WALKER, Leo. *Wonderful Era of the Great Dance Bands* (Howell-North Books, Berkeley, California 1964)

and

Memory Lane (incorporating the Original 1930s Record Society and the Al Bowlly Circle) published by Ray Pallett, Memory Lane, 40 Merryfield Approach, Leigh on Sea, Essex, SS9 1NA

ACKNOWLEDGEMENTS

By far the greatest problem involved in a book such as this is the paucity of good and, more important original illustrations. After a careful study of other books on this subject I believe the final choice to be a reasonable blend of historically interesting, technically good, and non-hackneyed photographs of the leading personalities of big band music.

Many of these are from my own private collection assembled over the years, but I must thank, very sincerely, all the helpful people who contributed photographs from their own files and family albums in order to try and present a new slant on an over-exposed scene. I am grateful to old friends who rallied round—Robert Farnon, Alan Kane, Kenneth Pitt, Michael Kennedy of World Records Ltd, and David Hughes of Polydor Records Ltd; and to new friends that I have been happy to make in the course of writing the book— Mrs Joyce Stone, who shared her memories and photographs of her beloved Lew, Ray Pallett of *Memory Lane*, and Roger Dooner for whom Minneapolis wasn't too far. To them all my public thanks in addition to those expressed in person.

My gratitude particularly to Henry Hall who, although ill, found time to seek out and personally annotate pictures from his own files; to the Press Office of the Savoy Hotel, to whom the past is far from a closed book; and to Harry Leader, who still takes an interest.

Max Bercutt of Warner Brothers Pictures, Burbank; Brad McKuen and Frank Santano of RCA Victor Records, New York; and the London offices of 20th Century Fox Film Co Ltd, United Artists Corporation Ltd, Universal Pictures Ltd, Paramount Pictures (UK) Ltd, and Walt Disney Productions Ltd—their help on a previous project enabled my own files to accommodate the demands of this one. And, while it is impossible to name all the personnel in record company Press Offices who have been helpful during my twenty-five years as a record reviewer, I can credit the following for many of the photographs used: EMI Records Ltd, Decca Records Ltd, MGM Records Inc, Pye Records Ltd, Capitol Records Inc, and Phonogram Records Ltd, with a special thanks to Leonard Hibbs and Francis Antony Ltd for the loan of illustrations from *The Gramophone Record, Audio Record Review* and *Jazz Monthly*.

One final acknowledgement must be to Ron Goodwin, without whom the whole thing would never have happened.

INDEX